Jessica Ghazarian is a Lebanese-Armenian writer. She started writing as a hobby in 2002. She holds a Master's degree in cell biology from the University of Manchester, UK. She is working as a senior channel manager in the genomics field in UAE. She believes that life is simple and complicated, and both are critical assets required to grow and evolve. Jessica loves to run behind adrenalin, take risks, share love, and help people as this flourishes the mind and heart with a flying free soul.

Jessica Ghazarian

ECHO OF SURVIVAL

AUSTIN MACAULEY PUBLISHERS™

LONDON • CAMBRIDGE • NEW YORK • SHARJAH

ISBN – 9789948779926 – (Paperback)
ISBN – 9789948779933 – (E-Book)

Application Number: MC-10-01-4692229
Age Classification: E

First Published 2024
AUSTIN MACAULEY PUBLISHERS FZE
Sharjah Publishing City
P.O Box [519201]
Sharjah, UAE
www.austinmacauley.ae
+971 655 95 202

The author would like to thank her family and friends who have been encouraging her to publish her writings. Moreover, she is appreciative of her own life experiences as well as the people who gave her the creative inspiration to write the echo of survival.

Table of Contents

Dancing Soul

Loving you engulfs my heart with ecstatic emotions
Having to deal with you is what I want in life.
Kidnapping is a crime, but kidnapping your heart is a crime
that I want.
Dealing with problems is nothing whenever you are with
me.
Having thoughts about you make my heart shiver with no
regrets.
laughing about your silly jokes draws a smile on my lips.
Being with you is everything I wish for.
Living life without you would be a burden on my shoulder
Smelling your odor makes my heart pump fast expecting
your arrival.
Having a glance from your shiny eyes makes me lose
control.
Spending moments with you is all I need.
Crying with you makes my heart shrink and enter into a deep
sleep.
Dreaming about you makes my day full of joy.
Being close to you, explodes my emotions in a bizarre way.
You are in my thoughts, my heart, and my eyes.

You've captured me mentally and physically.
Loving you is the best thing to happen in my life.

It's the first writing written in 2002.

Loving the Negative Moments

The simplicity of life is to live, love, and enjoy. Precious moments leave their signatures in our memories.

Dating, friendship, and family live within the atmosphere of love and joy.

Our soul pretends to be keen to overcome the complexity of our mind and tries to dance within the inner happy emotions.

Sometimes the jealous thoughts inside the mind wake up to ruin the friendly positive dancing vibes floating in our souls.

It is not a shame to have those odd unconscious thoughts caused by our minds.

However, the most important is not to be controlled by them.

Life swims through positive and greedy negative moments.

Those greedy moments try to interfere, dominate and kill every decisive moment surrounding our life.

We must accept that life will hit us with an unpleasant event.

We must acknowledge that the beauty of life is to challenge our soul,

Think about it!

Imagine your life is always working the way you would like it.

How would you evolve? How would you adopt different thinking?

How would you overcome stress? How would you develop new ideas if the challenges do not push you to think out of the box to find solutions?

If that is the fact, your life will become routine, static, and emotionless because, in the end, you become immune to everything, and your immunity need not fight any negativity, or any obstacle, and with time, your freedom will die.

Our days should circle around positive vibes and should evolve around barriers that will enable our souls to become stronger.

Unconsciously, the obstacles will introduce excitement and challenge into our life.

From those obstacles, our minds and souls evolve.

Ambition is a word used by many people.

Many of those pretend to have a purpose and talk about it as if it is innate and buried in their daily life.

Surprisingly, some people misuse the word.

What ambition is? Try to think and take it to another level?

Ambition merely is the strength to take risks.

You might ask how?

Indeed, it is! Take an example; your goal is to reach high professional levels, to own a house, to own a sports car, to have a family, and to help people. This is ambition, but how does the dream become a reality?

How will it exist in your life? How will it engrave itself in your history and experience?

Simple! By taking risks. You might say OK; I understand, but how risks can bring ambition to life?

Example: My ambition was to own a Porsche; my risk is the finance with the big question what if I couldn't pay? My answer would be: you are smart enough with your self-confidence, your smartness, your past experiences, and your fearless personality, you can do it, take the risk and bring your ambition to life.

All those things are interconnected, it is like a loop.

Ambition, self-confidence, fearless, taking risks, and then the loop continues.

What I am saying sounds easy and straightforward, but ask yourself why you see so many smart people, who have great ideas and are ambitious but never accomplished great things in their life if they and their families are in good health.

Why not?

Because their ambition is limited to an abstract idea, limited to what their brain wants them to believe in and not spread to their actions, to their inner soul, which is fearless of taking risks and implementing their ambitions.

Always try to keep your life as positive as it is.

I have said this before and will repeat it, do believe that at the end of every negative moment, there are many positive ones and our moments always have a beginning and a closure no matter whether they are positive or negative.

Our life revolves around thousands of moments, but ultimately, all are born, and all are dead.

Indeed, those moments can be buried in our memories, but they are eventually doomed from our daily life.

Never think that life will always be so kind to you.

Be happy that it is not all the time great or else you would never evolve and learn.

Because of the obstacles, we are forced to think out of the box, and those thoughts bring new thoughts with them that are positive by nature.

Look to the past negative experiences you had, how many of those you think happened for some reason, and ask yourself: did those experiences make you stronger?

Those thoughts make us grow without realizing

In the end, accept that positive and negative moments exist in everyone's life.

Most important is how to handle those moments and turn them in-to lovely ones.

The most important is to believe that at the end of the tunnel there is always light.

Madness, Beauty, Heart, and Mind

Faith allows our soul to feel safe,
Confidence in the best of life enlightens our soul with happiness.
Too many unpleasant moments strike our days.
Too many unexpected madness grab our thoughts into its world.
There is a beauty behind all that.
Despite how awkward it might sound.
The attractiveness is to be kidnapped into the madness world.
Despite being trapped there.
The beauty is to keep on living neglecting the surrounding,
Ignoring all the surrounding madness, the amazing part is to own your world, while the madness has captivated everything around you,
Own the simple, lovely piece left that is trying to breathe despite the harshness introduced by the madness.
Own it with what's left of your soul and energy.
The soul that was born with only beautiful, lovely emotions,
The madness becomes jealous of the beautiful, pleasant feelings tanning the soul,
The madness is continually trying to invade the lovely

moments to leave its signature forever.

Despite all the tricky unpleasant acts the madness is causing to disrupt the beauty surrounding the SOUL.

The attractive, positive SOUL stays in the world of beautiful emotions and builds the thickest wall ever built in the entire universe

A wall protecting the incredible feelings inside this beautiful world, against all the madness.

Lovely how the heart changes its mood occasionally and often.

Lovely how the heart is egoistic to the point of not thinking about the mind,

Not thinking about all the efforts, the brain is trying to implement, to get rid of any complications that might affect our way of living.

However, these complications might be beautiful

Complications arising from love,

As soon as the heart falls in love, it becomes selfish,

As soon as it feels the beauty of the lovely emotions, and it locks the door in front of what is right or wrong.

At the same time, the mind tries to enter the heart's world,

Attempts to find a small hole in the heart's world to enter, and figures out why the heart has been acting in this bizarre, selfish manner.

No opportunity to discover this hole.

No chance to try and knock on the heart's world.

After all, reality has ruled,

The fact that the soul is living in the most amazing, lovable, and emotional world.

Self-control must be easy when the heart is entirely in a conscious state.

To be controlled by emotions is so easy when the heart is wholly in the unconscious state, the stage of love; at this stage, the job of the mind becomes dormant to the point it forgets it has ever existed.
Too many descriptions can be given; however, what matters, in the end, is the beauty arising from the selfish manner of the heart, just because it is locked by love.

Written on 24 June 2012.

Must Read, Just Life

Life is a word composed of four letters;
A tremendous meaning lies behind those four letters.
It is not important how many years we live;
The most crucial is what signature we leave behind us.
The choice of entering this life does not exist
But, the decision to live it in the best way lies within our
minds and soul.
Struggling in our everyday life is a must for us to survive in
this harsh world.
As if we are born only to fight.
Despite our everyday struggle, there are moments when we
empower ourselves with happiness
As if flying over the world with pureness fulfilling our body
and mind.
The moments we spend are worth the experiences.
Ignorance closes our road to success,
Our passions engulf us with power and love to drive through
this rocky world.
Freezing the silence found inside our heart sends us to a
deserted place with no chance to retrieve ordinary life;
Unreeling the silence inside our mind sends us to the deepest
place in the sea where the darkness captures us alive.
We are lucky to have a chance to experience life.

People are born with no troubles in their pockets.
In the first three years, the purity eats us like pieces that swallow a small fish;
The purity swims freely into our blood and organs.
Three years will pass;
Suddenly, we are thrown into the school
Wanting it or not, education will float into our souls and minds.
Building our knowledge is the essence of a successful life.
Fifteen more years will pass.
Now, the purity inside will be obliged to fade with time;
after those beautiful eighteen years, our eyes will open to the real world.
The desire to close them back and escape from reality is out of our hands
As if we are judged by it till the last moments of our lives.
Days are passing like the draining of water in the river,
Our journey in this world faces obstacles;
Overcoming those embraces us with power.
Surrendering is for weak people,
Years pass by quickly,
Nothing can stop it.
It cannot be followed or slowed down as if you are following your shadow.
Working hard is one of the crucial things that should be engraved in our minds.
Work opens our eyes to things never believed to exist.
We work hard to reach our goals; sometimes, we feel down emotionally and mentally.
In the end, getting up again on our feet and focusing on our target keeps us living; decisions are taken every single day.

Our decisions might be so silly, but ultimately in one way or another, they will matter.

No matter if you are rich or poor, just pay attention to the faces of people and try to visualize what is hidden behind their faces. Dig deep inside the person's soul and never think you are better or worse than him/her, no matter what.

Always be confident – a quality that protects you from being a prisoner for others.

Being betrayed is awful, but overcoming it pumps the power hidden inside, opens the door, and jumps into freedom.

Unexpected moments arrive, barge themselves inside our lives, leave us with no choice except to accept them and fill us with sadness as the harsh reward given to us.

Incredible moments exist, lived by us, and ended eventually; however, these memories will be engraved in our souls, history, and mind.

Our target in life is to be not lazy and to accomplish so many things.

No one of us knows the future;

Despite this, we see what life offers us.

Underestimating our capabilities would be as having a lack of self-confidence.

All of us always search for the treasure, no matter what it is,

Our treasure is deep inside, which is more potent than anything else.

DON'T BE AFRAID OF THE UNKNOWN; BE SCARED OF BEING FEARFUL OF THE UNKNOWN.

Trust yourself, because after all, no one knows you more than yourself.

We are always struggling to have a good life; it is like

swimming in the sea with a known destination; however, it needs time for you to reach.

Sometimes we say, "Enough," we can't handle it anymore; we enter a weak moment, which is no shame.

Each one of us experiences this moment, and it is essential not to be shy about it;

Believe it or not, stupidity lies in each person.

Power to manage and keep it in the dark shadows and out of the light will prevent us from being eaten by some monsters.

Always fill your cup with strength;

Leave no place for fear.

After all, the power and energy will allow us to conquer the world.

Written on 12 May 2009.

Spreading Positive Energy

We are thrown into this universe for a purpose. We have a tendency sometimes to ask ourselves; what is our mission in this life?

Some people live their lives without realizing their purpose of living.

Some people, once their happy moments are struck by negativity, they start working on their existence in this life.

My most important purpose in life is to open a charity and help people ultimately.

Spreading positive energy should be embedded in our mission in life.

How to do that? Support people morally, provide them with positive energy and motivation to overcome their problems, and help them excel in business.

Support might be anything, like maybe just a chat, perhaps they want to share their thoughts, relax and feel that someone is listening to and feeling them.

Being able to draw a smile on someone's face is a fantastic thing we can do.

Being able to share positive energy with people who have been feeling down or have problems is an ecstatic thing that drives my days.

Sometimes, our energy goes down; it is OK, but always remember even a small smile, and small support can lift someone morally.

It is incredible how your ideas and positive energy can encourage others to start thinking the same way.

To encourage others that there is way more in life than just living it. The positive energy that is walking with you during the day and incorporating itself into your time without taking permission from you is the best feeling.

While it's true that sometimes we feel down or sad, yet the positive energy that has been built over the years cannot be withdrawn forever.

It has buried itself in our souls, buried itself in our minds and lives.

I love the fact that we can provide such support and energy to others.

It draws our life with happiness and reflects on our souls with more positive energy.

I have met people with problems that are so bad to the point that it affects their lives tremendously.

It is incredible when you hear a person saying, "I am happy I hear your voice. You give me energy." It is great when you feel that you can change someone's mood by just being with them or chatting with them.

The toughest part is that people keep expecting you to be positive all the time, but it is OK as long as you leave a good impact.

Friends or even strangers opened up to me over the years.

I have witnessed people telling me their deepest secrets in less than a few hours of knowing me.

I have had people who told me about the darkest of the darkest moments they have lived or are living.

I have had people telling me they want to get divorced.

I have had people telling me their family history was full of misery and heartfelt problems.

It is not easy to hear those stories because they are sad and negative, but at the same time, it seems they feel comfortable telling them; it appears that our positive energy provides them with some relief and trust that we do not judge. We don't know what it is for them to open up so quickly, and we don't even know what it is in us that allows them to feel chilled and trust us so fast, but we love it.

I am in love with the fact that we can provide relief to people who always wanted to talk or want to talk.

We should not shy ourselves from opening up to others.

Life is simple.

If I said that dark moments do not exist, then I would be lying to myself.

Life does include dark moments, moments where we are not able to think anymore, and where we are not able to live in the moment because our mind is being pulled into the deep, pulled to the point where it sees only darkness.

However, the best part of all this is the outcome when the darkness turns into lovely moments.

As I always say, nothing lasts forever; at the end of the tunnel, there is always light.

Within our deepest darkness, our soul should always know that there is light at the end.

Yes, it can take days, but in the end, everything has a solution.

It is fine to feel sad, it is fine to struggle, and it is fine to face problems because if we do not, then we would not grow.

If we do not, we would not be able to overcome the next obstacle.

Life should not always be perfect; probably, it is stupid to say this, but it should not.

I am not saying that it should always be harmful, and there is a level of badness someone can tolerate.

However, living through dark moments provides us with the strength to strive and grow.

It gives us a new vision of life and makes us appreciate the pleasant moments we have.

Experiences are always worth living and having, no matter what type it is.

I always say, our moments are like a product that has a beginning and an end.

Whether they are bad or good ones, if they start, they will definitely end, and a new one will begin.

This is our life, and that is how we learn and evolve.

With dark moments we can build a wall for future miseries.

This wall will be our safety shield because, due to our past experiences, we have built it, and we became stronger so that the next problem thinks twice before it knocks on our door and gives us a harsh time.

Life is simple, and we need to believe that it is not always perfect.

Our strength allows us to survive.

Written on 9 October 2018.

Patience and Hope for
a Better Career

Work is essential to survive in this rocky world. Ambitious minds always crave a successful professional career.

The eager minds want a prosperous professional career.

Most human beings are employees and have to work under certain conditions.

Dictatorship is found in most careers, whether at the level of a manager, company management, and/or colleagues.

The question is, how can we survive in such a world?

Simple: We need to have ambition, the mindset of changing, and hope for a better future.

I have witnessed many friends, family members, and colleagues loving and hating their job.

The mixed feelings are born because of the manager, company salary packages, rights, and career development.

Sometimes we love our job, but we hate our manager.

Other times, we love our manager but hate the company or colleagues.

Ultimately, we rarely find a great mix of loving the job, the manager, and the company.

Looking at my friends' experiences, most of them hate going to work and staying after working hours.

How to encourage them?

Again, everything has a beginning and an end.

Having a bad job is just a phase, as long as motivation and determination are there to find a better one.

Take it with hope. I know it is not easy to go to work when it makes you feel unhappy and turn your days into nightmares.

Or you hate the atmosphere.

Or you feel you are a slave to others.

Or you feel mistreated or abused.

Or you just hate your manager but love your job.

Think about it differently.

True, it is hard to wake up every day to go to work.

Indeed, you want this to end.

But trust this: determination and ambition for a better career will abolish those bad days.

Again, you will be waking up in a depressed mood, with the feeling that you are not accomplishing anything in your life, of being controlled by other people, of being in prison, with the belief there is no hope, and this is going to last forever.

Trust me; this will not last forever. Whether or not you are going to stay for a bit longer, eventually, every phase in your life has a beginning and an end.

Many people are facing the same dilemma.

You are not alone; never think that you are the only person.

However, what differentiates you from other people is the hope, patience, ambition, and determination you have to find a better job without surrendering.

Believe in one thing: it is meant to happen.

Believe in one thing: despite the harsh moments you are having, ultimately a fantastic opportunity will hit your life, and you will say to yourself:

"Wow, I am a strong person."

"Wow, I was able to stay in that job despite everything, and I did not quit until I found this new career that I am in love with."

I am not saying this just to say it, but I have experienced it.

I know what it means to hate going to work.

I know how it feels to wake up every day with the idea of going to work.

However, with my determination, I stood there, and I conquered the days.

Right, I decided to leave that career; true, I said I could not survive there.

However, I stayed until I found another job.

In the end, I ended up believing more in the patience I have.

You will look at that phase and say, "We do have to pass through rocky moments to become stronger and know how to deal with shit."

All you need to believe in is the hope for a better future. This will make you more reliable and ultimately oblige you to go and search for the best job rather than sticking to this one.

However, I would like to mention something essential.

Such a thing cannot be accomplished if ambition, hard work, and a mindset to change do not exist in our daily life.

Things never come on their own.

Things never knock on our door without us seeking them.

I did not mean just anything; I said the best things in life.

Things will eventually change, and as long as you trust yourself that you are going to change them for the better, then they will change for the best, not even better.

Just have patience, and it is not shameful to be sad, and it is not shocking to be unhappy with your job.

It is not shameful to go and tell your friend, "I am not happy."
However, keep the positivity in your mind.
Keep a space for positivity, and do not allow yourself to sink into the negative moments.
Let the negative moments be there; however,
embrace the positivity more and keep hope in the fact that the best is yet to come.
Slowly, slowly all those negative moments will vanish, and only positive things will surround you.
Just keep hope and self-confidence for the existence of a better future.

Mindset

People's actions and levels of success are an **outcome** of a type of mindset.

A positive mindset revolves around self-confidence and a love of taking risks to achieve one's dreams.

A negative mindset revolves around a fear of failure and avoiding taking action for a change, which may lead to a hole in life.

For many people, the risks are considered a dark, mysterious path that might eventually fail.

As such, this is a negative mindset; sadly, it is shared by most people nowadays.

We need to understand that anything we do in life revolves around risks.

Unlike more traditional thinking, risk-taking should be embedded in our souls.

Now, you might ask me: how come you are considering risks to be the soul mate of our soul?

Think about it. Why are some people who were born poor able to succeed and excel in life while others did not, taking into consideration all actions are legal?

It is because the heart, mind, and soul are filled up with the passion to excel using all inner powers and love that taking risks will enable these ideas to become a reality.

Remember, at the end of the day: no risk means no success, which means no learning from failure, which means no development, and eventually means ending up with regrets at the end of this life.

As an example, my path started from scratch, and it was not easy as there are things in life we cannot control; however, the things we can control should embed into our positive mindset.

I have highlighted some events in my life in this book just to show how everyone can do it.

There is no difference between me and any other person. Everyone can do it as long as the health of everyone around them is good.

How can a positive mindset lead to changing your life toward the best in every moment?

Since forever, I have wanted to study abroad but had no financial resources to achieve that.

But within the deep parts of my heart, soul, and mind, I kept the idea floating in a silent volcanic way without projecting it to the outside world.

Floating within this, I was so determined that one day I would study abroad.

My mind and heart focused on working a lot to save money.

I was called many times a very stingy person, with no sense in other people's minds of why I was not spending money.

For them, it was stupid and stingy not to spend money, but I swallowed every bit of that feedback and continued my journey to one destination: studying abroad.

I believed that a degree from abroad would be a signature that would stay forever in my life and would allow me to reach high levels.

Thank God I was able to accomplish this dream despite all the different obstacles I faced, from having no money to my grandma's death.

But at the end of the day, I got the result I craved.

Three years after graduation, I was able to move to Dubai with a job that I knew. I would not love but was an essential step toward the future I was aiming to have.

The road was not easy, and moving along the path, many adverse events hit my way toward achieving my ambition.

Despite all of that, one mindset was dominating my life.

The mindset that I can do it. The mentality of achieving my goal.

I got hit by rocks that wanted to crack my positive thinking, but no one knew or understood that we, and only we draw our main path, and so I did. Passing down that path was great because I built a thick wall around it.

How to describe my path:

My path is a long bumpy road. I have built a rough road just to learn from it.

The ultimate destination is my dream.

A thick wall built by me surrounds the path.

Those walls could never collapse because they represent my confidence, ability to thrive for success, love of taking risks, and life; most importantly, my HUMBLENESS.

Someone told me that the difference between self-confidence and ego is when someone loses their humbleness trait.

Back to the wall, I have built for many years:

The only way those walls could collapse is because of me and ONLY ME.

The thick walls have protected my path from all the thunderstorm outside.

The negativity has initiated the thunderstorm, the negativity caused by people around me trying to diminish my dreams, lower my confidence, and flourish the path with jealousy.

Back to the bumpy road along the path within the protective walls: despite all negativity the thunderstorm is bringing, I should say that I like such storms.

Why? Just because of the fact they can hit me with challenges that can bring excitement to our life.

A challenge is something that triggers the mind and heart to run with the adrenaline rush.

Surprisingly, we are intrigued by many things in life that bring challenges.

At one point, we might get scared and run away with all our souls. But at other points, we fall in love with the fact that the challenge is capturing our full alertness to win or overcome it.

A challenge could be something simple, but, at the same time, could be a battle by itself.

The challenges are there to improve our vision of life.

The challenges are there to make us smarter.

The challenges are there to make us think outside the box and stay away from the routine.

The challenges are there to provide us with the confidence that risks are the best thing in life.

They are the second part of our soul, for which we need to feed on them.

Without taking risks, our soul will become older than its real age.

Our souls will end up alone and will die with a sense of enormous regret.

Never allow that to happen. Trust your smartness, trust the fact you know what you are doing, and trust the fact that you are studying your path well before drawing it and building a very thick wall around that path. Believe that even in the worst cases if you failed to achieve what you wanted—or let me frame it a different way if you were not able to reach the end destination—then trust that road has taught you a lot in your life for your next chapter. Then, at least you have tried and tried very hard, without being afraid of that path and the risks. Now, let me come back to what happened after the job I got in Dubai.

I aimed for the dream job I had always wanted, a sales position in a big principal biotechnology company.

However, who would have thought the biotechnology company would be Thermo Fisher Scientific, a 70,000-employee worldwide company worth $22 billion? There was me competing against many applicants not only coming from prominent companies, not only based in Dubai with regional experience, but also with those wanting to move from abroad to Dubai, both from out of Thermo and within Thermo.

In the end, it worked out.

Now, I entered Thermo without anything.

All I had were debts and debts, in the UAE and Lebanon.

The path that I have drawn was protected first and foremost by my self-confidence.

My self-confidence is in the fact that if I want something, I can work hard to achieve it.

As long as the health of my family and me is good, nothing can compete with that at all.

My ambition was protected with my trust,

My trust in the best of life,

My belief that life is not all about positivity, but

also negativity and that sometimes, it is excellent to be bombarded with negativity to learn and develop,

My trust in the fact that negative moments are born but also will die after a while.

My trust in the fact that the end destination of every dream is walked through only with my self-confidence and faith in the best of life,

It was protected by my passion for aiming high enabling me to open a charity at the end of the day.

My passion is to thrive and try to provide positivity to people in need,

To try and show those people what the purpose of the different moments occurring in our life may be.

It was the year 2018, when my debts improved.

It was the year when I had taken a huge decision that was so risky for many people, but I believed I can do it.

Now, after almost two years, I would still take the same decision. If it fails at one point, I would know at least I tried.

Around mid-2018, a crazy idea bombarded my life and thoughts, the idea of buying a car.

Well, a used Porsche.

With my lack of patience, my crazy mind went and told me to buy a new one, with no need to waste time.

The story of that car is in this book, so I will only describe it briefly here.

Many people said, "Jess, it is so crazy! What are you doing? Why on earth would you spend so much money on a brand-new car?"

All I was thinking of was, "What is the risk? The risk would be to lose the car and thus money. If so, then why not? I could always say I had bought a brand-new Porsche and driven a brand-new Porsche, and accomplished a dream."

And there it was, I have taken a decision, and now I am driving a 2018 Porsche.

Days passed by and my life kept on improving. I believe this because of my love of taking risks, strategizing, and drawing the next path of the following dream (or two dreams) at once.

Another goal was born, to be accomplished on my March 2019 birthday, which is nine months after the Porsche.

The dream was to buy a Rolex on my birthday.

Unbelievably, during that period, many things were precarious.

A strong storm hit me.

The walls of my path got hit by a strong storm, even though the storm did not affect my way or my mindset and confidence in that path, the blast shook the walls very severely.

But at the end of the day, if plan A does not work then plans B, C…are always there. Those plans are created by my self-confidence that I can survive this storm with my hard work and patience.

Days, and months passed by, and the strength of the storm was getting stronger and moodier.

It was sometimes dormant, sometimes hitting again.

At one moment, I told myself, "Do not buy this watch.

No need for it now; keep some cash because, in the worst case, you do not want to sell your car at least for eight months and want to live comfortably."

There it was: that thought that covered my 14 days until the last week before my birthday.

I felt a burden on my head. I thought that a big building was just standing on my head.

It was there to tell me that what I decided on, namely not buying the watch, would prove that what I had been thinking and believing in was just a lie, and it would prove that I am not truly a risk-taker and it would show that I have low self-confidence in setting the path of my life. So with all those thoughts roaming around, just four or five days before my birthday, I decided to buy the watch.

The time the decision was taken was the time when I was relieved from a significant burden.

It is the time when I kept my promise and was not afraid of failure.

So 8 March 2019, was the day when I owned the watch.

I always say: these days might die. I always say: all of this does not mean

I will for sure still be able to buy what I want, but it means one thing: ACCOMPLISHMENTS.

But I also always say: being proactive in life is key for a continuous future.

Rich people can become poor and vice versa. Life is like a wheel that always rotates: you can keep it sometimes at a specific position, but to be able to do that, you have to trust in the best of you and life.

Now, I will leave this writing until the next accomplishment and the subsequent path drawing.

Written on 31 July 2009.

Turning 31

March 8, 2018, the day I turned 31.
Humans tend to fall in love with their birthdays during the initial years.
The day we feel we are turning 30 is the day when we engage in this weird misconception that we are turning 30 and becoming old.
30! OMG! When did this happen?
Since I turned 30, I decided that big decisions will be taken and accomplished on every birthday from 30 till 40.
On my 30th, I went skydiving, and it was the hit of my life.
On my 31st, 8 March 2018, I signed off documents for something big.
Those documents are prerequisites for a vast and bright future.
I have made a decision and promised myself that by 35, I would be a big businesswoman starting with significant investments.
I am writing this not to show off and brag, but it is to encourage people to do the same, to support everyone educated or not educated to do the same.
Life is a story of adventures.
To think differently is a loss of what the future would be.

To think similarly is a tremendous success of where the days will take you.

Humans have a tendency to say it is risky, I am scared, I cannot take the risk

Years to pass by, and the same words come out of most people's mind.

It is risky, I cannot make the decision.

What if I fail?

I would say who cares, let it not work because of this, you will learn and succeed better in the upcoming decision.

Why do people become scared of making decisions?

I would say it is all about self-confidence. If you believe you can succeed in accomplishing what your mindset on, then you take the decision. If you think you have a bit of risk but deep down, you have the power to accomplish what you set on achieving, then go for it,

It is the power found inside us, either we release it, or we bury it inside.

Taking Risks and Porsche Experience at Age 31

An idea that has always been a dream.

An idea that has always been related to emotions. BUYING A SPORTS CAR, A PORSCHE.

My emotions started communicating with my brain to reach high alertness, saying I need it.

During this time, there was a big dilemma happening in my mind:

Buy, don't buy, buy…the dream had lain there dormant for years since I was young. Buy! You love sports cars. Buy, you are in UAE.

On the other hand, don't buy it. You don't need a new one, go INVEST.

However, the power of emotions, mind, self-confidence, and love of taking risks pushed my mind to the STUBBORN state of getting the PORSCHE ASAP.

A plan to buy a used Cayman Porsche had begun.

The search started; the green button had been pushed.

Before continuing, I would like to say.

Things happen for a reason!

Actions and the right decisions are required, NO FEAR OF TAKING RISKS.

I always say, "RISKS are constant daily partners for most human beings."

The fear of taking risks loves to dominate our mental state and our life. Success will never reach us as long as the fear of taking risks keeps controlling our lives.

Human beings have a tendency to wear a safety shield around their life whenever they feel a risk is approaching.

Back to my Porsche story,

I saw a used Cayman 2014. I did not feel it was the right one due to some things the owner mentioned.

During this time, the idea grew more and more and became more influential to the point of explosion, to the point of getting it now, to the point of something I would call CAR BUYING ADDICTION.

Stubbornness hit an all-time high, shooting beyond my capacity to wait and maintaining patience affected me a lot.

The stubbornness of getting a Porsche,

The determination of getting a Porsche ASAP,

I went to Ras Al Khor; I searched for a car on dubizzle, but again my patience was nonexistent.

Stubbornness and having no patience can sometimes be positive.

So, I went to the Porsche showroom for the first time to check for a used car, and I was like OMG so expensive, and left.

I went to the Porsche showroom for the second time to ask their opinion about second-hand and detailed information. I got frustrated because the dream of buying a car woke up inside my mind and was not only an emotional thing; my soul woke up this dream. I was Jessy, no time for a used car, only a new car. I told myself, you can do it! Just set a plan for how to pay the fees, and you will for sure do it. What is the risk?

Worst case scenario, you will sell the car, and lose some money, but the beauty would be you DROVE A PORSCHE 2018 in 2018 brand new, you accomplished your Dream, took a risk, and ultimately have NO REGRETS.

The decision had been made, the mind had been set, my emotions became very excited, and the time came to go to PORSCHE for the third time.

Before going again to the showroom, I decided on my maximum budget.

Only 12 days had elapsed since that moment I decided to move forward.

The day had come to go to Porsche with my friend. My heart was beating so fast, parked the car, and I looked at the PORSCHE sign, and said, "Wow, I am going literally to buy a Porsche 2018 brand new."

I entered hoping I can find a basic option, Cayman 2018.

Shockingly the price for the 2018 Cayman was a full option, 20k dollars more.

While sitting there with my friend, a volcano of thoughts erupted inside my mind:

This is so expensive! Why don't they have a basic model? I don't need all of these options. Jessy, this is too much, your initial budget for a used car was way lower, this is more than double.

However, on the other hand, my emotions were saying, it is only money. What will happen in the worst-case scenario?

You only live once, you can do it, you can pay without losing money, and most importantly you love sports cars. It has been your dream since a young age, to take the risk (the best beauty in life is to take risks and say yes I have done it, and yes I have succeeded or worst case I have failed, but I have tried and no regrets).

I just did not want to make a quick decision based on emotions. So, we went home with the idea that it was too expensive.

I fell asleep at 1:30 am on June 11, and my thoughts were overwhelming. I know I take risks and love risks as if I am in love with risks; however, that night, all I was thinking of before sleeping was not to make a decision based on emotions and that this was an expensive car.

During the day on Monday, 11 June 2018, I decided, and I texted my other friend to see if she could meet me at the Porsche showroom at 10 am on Tuesday, 12 June 2018. She said yes and got excited.

I told her I might buy the car, and that I would bring a deposit just in case I did.

I arrived at the showroom and waited a bit for her.

I knew I was going to buy the car. I was like, "I am done."

I asked her to sit in the driver's seat, and she did, and she said, "Wow."

I asked, "What do you think of the color?"

She said, "Amazing." Then, when she turned the car on, she was so impressed and said, "Jessy, you need to buy this."

And I asked, "Are you sure?"

She said, "Yes."

I turned to the guy—I was in the passenger seat—and with a big smile on my face, I said, "Sold." That was one of the best moments in my life, and this was the moment I just accomplished a dream, the formalities of signing the contract, applying for a car loan, and picking up the car are pleasant but saying sold was beyond.

I am writing this with pride.

It is impressive how we set dreams and achieve them one by one. Confidence! Confidence that you are smart enough to take action, to weigh the advantageous and disadvantageous. Not to only love taking risks but to be in love with taking risks, and to understand that life is not all about winning.

Losing is essential, and without it, we cannot develop and evolve to become better.

It doesn't mean it always has to be a loss; once we accept that we are human beings and there is no harm in losing, no harm in failing because eventually, it is always better to lose rather than not trying and regretting it in our old age.

I don't want to reach a point in my life where I say, "I wish I did." Always listen to yourself.

Believe in yourself.

Believe that once you set your eyes on a dream that you can ac-accomplish it because you are smart, strong, and confident enough to set plans and actions toward your success.

For me, a dream is always nearby, waiting for my green light. I always felt I had this mental power state that I can achieve my dream. It is only me who can decide, it is only me who might be scared of risks, it is only me who can be affected by others' negativity, it is only me who draws my success, me and only me.

The only things that can stop someone from accomplishing their dream are health and death.

Out of all these, humbleness, love and respect for others, support for people, and other things should always and always should be there.

Never have an ego; people are all on the same level.

Friends told me, I should be proud of myself because this is a significant achievement, be careful of others, of new friends, of guys, life will change. I still cannot understand or probably don't feel that my life will change, but in one way or another, they are right; it is not us who change, but others might change toward you.

A few days before renting this apartment, my aim was one thing: to find a two-bedroom apartment, meet new people, and save money. An agent who was supposed to find me a two-bedroom decided to show me a three-bedroom.

Now, I feel I have accomplished so many dreams, my master's degree from one of the top 30 universities in the world, working at one of my dream companies, and now a Porsche, not forgetting helping others (best feeling ever).

Life is SHORT.

We always say it but never take it seriously.

I wish people trusted themselves more rather than what other people think of them.

My dad always told me since I was very young, "When you grow older, you will buy a Porsche, and I will sit next to you."

It feels so good now that I have made the decision.

It is all about positive thinking, self-confidence, and taking risks. Let us see what life brings next.

Written on 21 June 2018.

Living the Sharing Life in Apartment 6706 in Dubai

At the end of an era at Princess Tower, 6706, I am very proud of myself for having taken such a decision at a young age, and I always encourage my friends not to be afraid of anything and to just go for it because they are smart enough to make it work and succeed. Here you go: how this story got from renting two to three bedrooms.

I and the agent were in the elevator which was going up and up and up, to a place I did not believe would create amazing times and memories.

Life around that high-floor apartment was enormously unbelievable.

Going back to this elevator and after a few seconds, it stopped at the 67th floor. The whole viewing was beyond incredible, a phenomenal view.

The view included the full palm, Jumeirah Beach Residence, and Burj Arab.

Imagine you enter an apartment—an empty one—but still, get amazed in a bizarre way.

What added more to the beauty was that tiny balcony, which became part of my room.

The balcony that introduced many moments into my life,

The balcony that encompassed many talks,

The balcony that created the big project,

The balcony that introduced happiness to many strangers,

That view from that balcony just flourished people's minds and hearts with astonishment.

The view for them probably would never be seen by their eyes again.

That tiny balcony. Who would have thought it could bring so much into my life? Again, going back to entering the apartment.

I walked step by step. All I was thinking of was, "Do not fall for this apartment. Do not; you are here just to check the view and leave. Better say 'Run away from that' and 'Do not fall in love with it.'"

But OMG, the time I stepped on that balcony, was the time my mind and heart clicked together, saying,

"Take this apartment, take it. Do not think twice."

The view is beyond explainable.

I sat for hours on that balcony, just chatting and admiring the fantastic view.

Imagine you were on the 67th floor when the tallest you have been before was maybe 20 floors.

Today, 1 September 2019, after two years, I am sitting on the same balcony. My last time writing regarding what I am feeling and thinking, admiring for the last time the view—the view that brought so much comfort and admiration to many people and me.

So, I decided to rent the apartment. Jessy, the crazy Jessy, got obsessed, and what do I do when I get obsessed about something? I just take action. I accept taking the risk.

The days went by, and my preparations to enter the apartment started. My friend, who is not living here anymore, moved in with me, and I started searching for tenants.

At the same time, my heart and mind could not believe the view.

I hope I can remember the names of all the people who stayed for a long-term stay.

Here we go: Nadim, Mahmoud, Thomas, Selin, Daisy, Elham, Pedro, Markus, Wael, HK, Marcel, Tom, Tatiana, Megan…the rest were just people who were coming and going, but a lot.

Incredible how life is: one decision to check the view ended up allowing me to meet so many people who mostly became my friends.

Indeed, for the first time in my life, I kind of became the landlord. But to whom I am lying? I never felt I was a landlord. Instead, I became close to many of the tenants.

I could not back up from having a conversation by trying to bring excitement to them from living here.

Those days were filled with many parties with my friends. Emotions were roaming around all over.

Emotions were mostly happy.

Even if sometimes the apartment vibes went down, this was part of life, which went right.

However, 2 September 2017, was the first day of moving in.

The walls were naked of any happy emotions.

But all started changing, as soon as we filled up the apartment.

The walls started writing a history of all the moments lived there.

The walls were so excited to see what was next,

To feel the excitement and comfort people were bringing

A few times, a storm of negativity bombarded the atmosphere. However, the walls reimbursed their power to keep that real life.

Two new years were spent there. During the two years, my life was going through many good changes.

However, believe it or not, I do not regret any moment of those two years.

What can I say? Everything in life has a beginning and an end.

I do not regret that I rented this apartment.

It made me grow on all levels.

But the era has ended now, today, with me sitting on the same balcony that made me fall in love with this apartment.

The balcony, which is so tiny that it could only fit a table and two people around it, had brought so many memories and positivity.

True, I have spent time on the balcony with people that I lost as friends. But those people have added to my life many things and made me grow into a different perspective.

OMG, you have to know how many stories were told on this balcony, well in the whole apartment.

I am sure I am not doing the apartment justice because the reality is beyond explainable.

I want to continue writing, but I feel that I cannot, due to the many memories I have in my mind and heart.

I am not sure how to continue.

All I know is that those two years cannot be summarized in two pages. Those two years have written history into my life. But now, it is time to flip this chapter and move to another one. Who knows what this new chapter will bring?

All I know and am aware of is that the history of those times has engraved itself in the minds and hearts of not only me but many other people who have lived here and felt at home.

It was indeed a home for those hearts and minds.

Now, it is 23:09, 1 September 2019, time to leave this balcony and apartment.

Believe it or not, I wish I could take this view and balcony/apartment with me, but I cannot.

Note that my saying that does not mean I am not in love with my new apartment.

The new apartment is another puzzle from my life's portrait; it is filling the picture and a great making puzzle.

Dear 6706, thank you a lot for introducing all those people to me and for all those memories.

Dear life, thank you so much for allowing such opportunities, and for introducing me to such opportunities, or maybe for allowing me to create most of the possibilities.

I have to highlight one important point: many people told me not to take the apartment.

"So many rooms! How will you bring the tenants? You will, for sure, lose money."

I am so happy I did not listen to them.

I am so happy I listened to my mind and heart.

My mind and heart were dancing out of happiness during those two years and enjoying the moments.

The apartment brought success, brought internal development, brought new people to my life, brought experiences, and tattooed moments in my memory.

Goodbye is calling me now.

Goodbye to all of these: goodbye to 6706, to Princess Tower, and welcome to my new apartment.

It is an emotional moment.

Here it is: now I am leaving this chair, taking a last view at night from this balcony, and saying my goodbyes until we meet again, after a year, with a new experience to write about. Goodbye.

Friendship Battling Death to Stay Alive

Friendship is a word used so often to the point that it is becoming a cliché in this world.

There is no borderline between utilizing the friendship word as a real or a beneficial one.

True friendships are built on the basis of trust, love, and commitment for better days.

To have a very close friend means to have a sister or a brother where nothing can ruin the lovely memories and moments.

Friendships can be great but at the same time toxic.

Sometimes negativity builds up, and you will be having two types of thoughts toward your closest friend.

A thought which says, I want to keep this friend despite what we are passing through.

Another thought would be, I do not need this in my life, it is causing me so much discomfort and ruining my lovely moments.

It is hard when two thoughts exist in your life toward a particular friend. Friendship evolves around two people who share experiences, laughter, bad moments, arguments, trust, support, and many other things.

The big dilemma is when a friendship starts fading away.

Trying to keep what is left from the friendship is hard, but not impossible.

During our friendship, we tend to ignore the things that disturb us in our friend.

It reaches a point where those disturbing things invade our mind, invade our memory, invade our heart and reaches a point where we cannot ignore them anymore.

Two things could happen.

We explode, or we communicate

Either way, the moment has to come for the big question: Can someone stay with close friends at the detriment of his/her comfort?

People can enter a state of mind where they are not sure if they want this friendship or not,

To decide to stay with close friends or lose the friendship is tough.

You know that you want to stay with close friends but at the same time, the current overwhelming negative moments the friendship is facing are tough to the point they have wrapped your heart with negativity toward that friendship,

Covered your lovely emotions that are buried in your heart toward your friend with a death-sentenced dooming the friendship.

These overwhelming negative moments have suffocated the positive memories to the point where you start working on walking away from this friendship as it has ripped every last beautiful moment left.

I do not want this friendship anymore is the only thing roaming in your mind.

However, despite all this, your beautiful emotions buried in the deepest secretive locations in your heart are fighting back those negative ones,

Lovely moments spent with that friend; pleasant moments that formed connective family bonds where disconnecting might take ages despite all the negative moments and hardships this friendship is facing.

True as I always say, things happen for a reason.

These things happen for us to grow, for us to learn from them, for us to see the other side of the world.

You can reach a stage where you know you are upset, you know you cannot handle this anymore, you know that you want to go directly to your friend and say everything, but then the big dilemma is when your mind starts going many ways

Your mind is saying, wait and give your friend a chance to prove that he or she cares

Your mind is telling, talk to your friend and sort it out from your heart. Your mind starts feeling more and more the pressure coming from the effect of negative thoughts toward this friendship.

Here is the golden question, does your comfort or friendship comes first?

Life is harsh sometimes. It puts us in circumstances where we want to take a particular decision, but we don't so that we don't hurt someone else

Our best option is to stay away from our friend for a while; however, if we do, our friend might notice, and our friendship will melt and fade away.

If we do not follow our best option, then we will keep feeling hurt from what our friend has done

Communication has always been the most durable bullet someone can throw toward any occasion.

We would love to mention the reasons behind our anger but in some particular situation, our friend might not understand those reasons and can go extreme.

The best option would be to build a wall between our lovely positive memories connected to the roots of our heart, and the negative thoughts that spread through around our mind all the way.

Time will reveal; however, most importantly, at the end have that communication with that friend.

Do that if that friend is worth keeping.

Keep it positive and defend the incredible moments if they are worth it with everything you have.

Calling Them Best Friends

eeting a new person could happen every day. Friendships tend to be born the moment two people connect and enjoy their time together.

Friendships start growing once trust enters the friendship world.

At that moment, the two friends become overwhelmed with the sweet moments they are living.

Overwhelmed with their importance in each other's lives.

With time, the friendship becomes stronger, builds a stable emotional connection, and surrounds those emotions with inscribed memories

Love is brought into our lives in different ways. There is love that is imposed by family.

This type of love cannot be escaped and is considered the most beautiful.

This type of love has no end and comes without condition

Love is expressed toward family, best friends, friends, and other people; however, being in love is a love expressed toward a lover.

Friends can become best friends to the point we consider them our siblings.

How often do we meet new people and consider them our best friends (BF)?

How often do we meet new people and view them as our BF,
but, in reality, they are just people we think are our BF?
Human beings tend to call many people their BF.
True, it is fantastic when we go party.
True, it is amazing when we spend time together.
However, deep down when it comes to negative moments,
When it comes to having personal problems,
When it comes to wanting someone to listen to our problems
and support us,
Wanting someone to be there, not only during the happy
partying times but also during our darkest moments.
This is when someone is considered a BF.
A real BF is someone that you can rely on, even if they are at
the end of the universe,
A real BF is someone that you can look into his/her eyes and
know what they are thinking or what you are thinking,
A real BF makes your soul feel free while talking to them.
A real BF is a friend whom you know whatever happens in
this universe and wherever you are, he/she would jump
immediately to be next to you and to support you from the
bottom of his/her heart
BF do become siblings.
Best friends are those you sit with while your soul dances on
every moment spent with them.
My best friend; you know who you are
Our friendship is old,
Friends for years,
Minutes became days,
Days became months,
Months became a year,
A year became years,

Years filled with joy and sadness
Years passed, and our friendship grew stronger.
Time has flourished our friendship with strong bonds
Our friendship has evolved around goodbyes.
For the past many years, we have not lived in the same country.
Our dreams at one point in life have separated us
But our friendship's strong bond always reunites us even for a few moments or days.
Friends are found in the happy and sad moments.
All my worries will fade whenever I have a chat with you,
You have been in my life for many years now.
Those years are filled with so many secrets, so many happy and dark moments.
I do not consider you a best friend anymore but rather a sibling who has become part of my family.
Now after several years, we still live in separate countries.
However, in the end with only one phone call or message, all my worries will melt.
It has been years and years since we became close,
Our minds and hearts have been buried in the deepest places of our memories dear BF. I am so proud of you and thanks for all the times you have been there for me even from far away.
As I mentioned, you are part of the family.

Complexity of Dating

Dating is brought into our lives suddenly.
The dating process is not easy
Along the way, two minds communicate together.
While other times, they collide in different ways.
The butterflies hibernating inside the soul wake up and start dancing in partnership with dating.
The excitement to receive a call, message, go on a date, and the prospect of a future makes dating an outstanding experience.
Sometimes, stubbornness hit the core of the dating beauty.
During dating, the heart becomes excited from the partner's whisper,
However, at the same time, it suffers when the call, message, or the hint doesn't knock at our heart's door, and when our partner starts disappearing slowly, slowly.
Bumpy roads exist during dating.
Bumpy roads exist without taking our permission.
Bumpy roads have been built by one or both partners.
The only question that lies behind every dating process is, why do sometimes people have to make it difficult when it is supposed to be smooth?
Because some people have no integrity to say sorry it's not working, or I'm just like you

Why one of the partners has to play games and show that he/she has the upper hand.

Stubbornness and ego to kill dating and the chance of creating beautiful moments.

Life is supposed to be smooth without complications.

Our mind has a tendency to complicate and over-analyze things that, in reality, never existed.

Dating is a complex process but also amazing.

In the beginning, most people play the game of you text me, play the game of I don't want to text him/her first; I don't want to sound that I like him/her; I have an ego to protect; I have the pride to show.

The worst part is when lies start floating and spreading into the dating atmosphere

Have the guts to say I like you or merely sorry, this is not working, and move on.

Why someone jumps from one date to another and keeps the old date hanging inside the loop of the dating life?

Why not just move on and stop hanging the other person as a plan B or C or D or even E?

Nevertheless, it is hard to ignore that dating is enjoyable, despite all the craziness it can bring.

Sometimes the madness that comes with dating is what, in reality, people enjoy the most.

The idea of not knowing what the other person is feeling or thinking, is the enthusiasm of not knowing.

However, the big dilemma is when the person sees and feels those games start to hurt his/her emotions but continue with the dating process.

Why? Is it because he/she cannot live alone?

Why? Is it because he/she loves attention, and needs to feed their ego with care?

Why? Is it because he/she enjoys swimming in the unknown?

I will leave this theme by just saying that dating is sought and loved by every soul, no matter how complex it can be.

Love

T**he sweet happiness.**
To be in love is an emotion expressed not often in our life,
It is the type of feeling that is not eager to enter our life very frequently, and
It is the type of passion that grabs the opportunity when the heart is weak.
The weakness caused by the lover's spirit spreading its spell on ours to own it.
To be in love introduces new emotions in our hearts.
The feelings that have been standing outside the door of our life for a long time.
The warmth with no sense of interfering or trying to knock on the door of our heart, until the right moment arrives.
The right moment where the world of the lover becomes fragile,
No strength to say 'No' to anything.
At this point, the sweet emotions enter smoothly,
Enter to overrule everything found,
Those lovely emotions are so kind, to the point that ignoring them becomes impossible.
Instead, embracing them in our hearts becomes the only thing to accomplish.

The heart has been waiting for such a moment to engulf these emotions into its world finally,
Engulf them with all the unusual dancing sensations they bring with them.
Incredible how lovely, shy, and sparkling emotions can change anyone's world upside down.
No matter how many obstacles try to kidnap the loveliness coloring our life.
Eventually, the purity of love destroys the madness coming from those harsh moments;
The purity of love does that without implementing any effort.
After all, the sweet, shivering emotions have left no place in our life and heart to be owned by any other passion;
These emotions are so selfish to the point that they enter our life and hold without any permission.

Written on 25 Nov 2013.

Wavy Emotions

Emotions, a combination of powerful elements. Emotions barge into our lives without taking our permission.

Emotions cannot be disregarded whatsoever.

The efforts implemented to control it are useless.

The ironic emotional situations permit us to increase our efforts,

The result of this is always unpredictable.

The circumstance by itself will determine to which extent we can control our emotions

To surrender, for your sentiments is no shame

To exceed the red light in surrendering traverses you to the danger zone.

The zone where you obey your feelings with no control to go back behind the red light.

To be in such a situation is terrible but the moments you live are worth all the badness.

To say that emotions can be under control all the time is a lie.

No matter what, emotional strength influences our way of living.

Emotion is a simple word loved and hated by many people.

Emotion is lovely how the heart is captivated by the power of emotions;

Emotions control too many situations in our lives.

At one point, we adore the beauty the feelings spread into our soul.

While at the other end, we just wished emotions never existed.

Why does our heart welcomes emotions at one end and tries to ignore them at another,

Why our heart can't embrace the different emotions knocking on its door,

Lovely, how we as humans try and control our emotions.

True that emotions kidnap our inner peace, kidnap our soul, kidnap what is left of our mind's existence; however, there are situations where we allow feelings to enter slowly into our heart to where we lose the battle with it, we lose all the conscious we had to fight the emotion back or to at least not allow it to dig its roots deep into our soul.

Do we usually have the courage to say no?

The courage to be harsh and close the door in front of the emotions that are lovely, but simultaneously, not lovely at that time of our lives our mind has an ego where it always tries to prove it is right.

It always tries to show our soul that emotions are a sign of weakness and in reality, sometimes emotions are not signs of weakness but signs of no control in our life.

We reach a point where the lovely feeling becomes a harsh reality,

We reach a point where the fantastic, beautiful moments we thought we are living, are something we never wanted to have.

Sometimes, our mind questions the emotions we experience

The same feeling we experience in a particular situation can, in reality, a few months down the line, be wrong and unexpectedly not what we thought.

People tend to forget that emotions are affected by our mood, the situation we are in, and the different circumstances we are in our life.

For example, sadness is a fact that hits our life occasionally. What differentiates one soul from another is how we can handle sadness. How much we can realize that the different emotions we are experiencing during that sadness period are genuine emotions or just unrealistic.

While we are sad, we can feel happy toward any attention given by anyone. We will sense the empowerment of the care and love given by that person. Emotions, breakups, and the questioned new emotion enter our life while we are still sad.

For example, breakups, most of the time, are harsh after any breakup or even during the breakup, the person tends to be vulnerable the heart is shocked, and enters deep silence, into deep sadness, into deep isolation.

The heart at that point is so susceptible to any new emotion to any attention given by a new person, at that time, the original excitement is questioned.

The soul learns to love and embrace the new feeling that is thought to be amazing.

However, the mind at that point wonders whether the new positive, lovely emotion is a real one or just due to the vulnerability of the heart; any feeling is a positive emotion.

As humans, we seek attention and new lovely emotions offered by any person at that point, while in a weak and vulnerable position, the heart cannot differentiate whether the new feeling is a nice real one or just believed to be authentic and embraces it until further notice.

Is the new positive feeling a real emotion of what we are feeling or only based on the deep silence?

Hibernating Heart

The heart that has been so sick since that day.
Sick of not being able to dance and fly with the lover's heart.
The heart becomes weak.
The lover's heart egoism induced my heart to hibernate
waiting for its return.
My body has missed my heart.
An enthusiasm was born since the first time my eyes were
attracted to an unknown lover
Too many ignorant moments strike our life leaving behind
ugly memories.
Too many ignorant moments are washed away the moment
our heart enters the world of passion.
Loving someone might awaken the stupidity factor found
inside.
The stupidity factor that is always living in a world of
dormancy in our life,
However, the heart's power can paralyze the body leaving
behind the stupidity
To love is not just to miss.
To love is not only to say I love you.
To love is to feel and sense the beauty of the heart
Dancing out of passion dancing bizarrely without caring

about anything else.

To love is to experience the enthusiasm surrounding the heart

To feel the charm emerging from this tiny sweetheart.

To say I love you is quite easy

But

To say I am in love with you is the passion by itself

At this point, reality hits our life.

The fact where we have to surrender and say

My heart is not mine anymore.

It belongs to someone else

So sweet to be in love

So sweet to the point that breathing becomes hard because the power of love that has invaded my life at the same time has ripped away all the normal functionality found.

It left behind the craziness but polished it with amazing shivering lovely feelings,

The feelings that shake whenever they encounter the lover at any moment. People can say I love you easily.

But the feeling of being in love does not hit our life occasionally.

One-Sided Love

The heart is essential for the survival of the soul.
We are humans, and in our nature, our emotions tremendously control us.
Emotions arise from the depth of the heart
However, the question is:
Can we decide how, when, and what to feel? Some people would say
Yes while others no.
Falling in love with someone or even liking someone badly!
Is it a feeling we control?
Can we say yes? We can control who we love or like?
If so, then love from one side does not exist.
It is known and believed by many people that the heart is so selfish to the point it does not take our permission before falling in love.
It has acquired a forever green light to love whoever it desires and chooses it does not care what the mind thinks.
Or whether or not the love we are feeling toward the person is reciprocal or takes into consideration the suffering we face.
At the same point, loving someone is the best thing that could ever happen.
On the other hand, having no control over who our heart desires and wants could be harsh on the soul.

This could leave our moments filled with what we call: Love from one side!

Most people consider loving from one side is very tough and would prefer not to experience it.

Personally, it is true that falling in love with someone who does not share the same feelings could be brutal on the soul and mind.

But look at it from a positive perspective.

Would you prefer to live life without experiencing this feeling, or would you love to embrace it with every single aspect it brings?

Loving someone is a special feeling that does not often knock our life,

For this reason, anytime it protrudes our soul in a harsh or lovely way,

The sentiments inside awaken a unique excitement in us.

It is a feeling that colors our life with beauty

From one point, we are loving, that person and enjoying those particular feelings.

While at the same time, the is this thing that is trying to abolish the lovely feelings felt even if it is from one sided love.

Consequences are consequences, and self-confident people can deal with such outcomes and enjoy the feelings.

However, all those dancing emotions inside and the thoughts are coloring our life.

True, our days would be filled with questions like:

Why does this person not feel the same?

Why did I have to fall for that particular person?

What if this person is in love with me but is pretending not to be?

How long will I keep feeling like this?

Many questions could rise; however, ultimately all we know
is that we are in love with this person.

We are in love, and our heart is pumping but pumping with
extra colorful emotions.

Some people bury this feeling in their hearts and soul.

While others just show it off with every aspect of it,
disregarding the consequences of such one-sided emotions.

Many people in this world experience one-sided love.

No rule says we have to fall in love with the person who is in
love with us.

We always forget the fact that there are people who have
fallen for us, but we did not fall for them.

We wish that we could fall for the person who falls for us

But this is not how the universe functions.

Nothing is perfect.

Ultimately, we should consider the best in everything and
thank life that it allowed us to feel such feelings.

Listening to the Heart or Mind After a Breakup?

It is unrealistic how sometimes our heart functions. Our heart, this sweet organ that keeps us alive, keeps our whole existence in this universe.

No idea, no words can describe it.

This organ turns into an ignorant, selfish state of existence. It denies the existence of the mind,

Works with all its power to fight the consciousness the mind is bringing to our life.

Call it selfish, call it stupidity, call it ignorance. It is what it is, a dominant controlling heart.

What initiates such actions? Love? Obsession? Purity? Is it the flow of dancing emotions?

Moments spent with the lover?

Moments hit our life without any prior notice.

At some point or to some point, we are mesmerized by the beauty expelled from those moments.

Are those moments livable forever?

Our mind would say and give a verdict of no, it's impossible.

However, our heart with its innocent face.

Like it or not, this is the best reality to have and live, but not forever. Have and live it to the point where the lover still lives under the umbrella of our heart and emotions.

The time when we need to take control is the time when it is not working anymore.

Are we supposed to suffer when things stop working? The answer is yes. But and I say but only temporarily.

It is a process.

Our heart at that moment has to reach a point where it becomes vulnerable in front of the mind.

To the point, it allows the mind to take control.

The lovely moments spent should not be erased; instead, they should be engraved in a unique location inside the heart and locked with a key owned by the mind.

The only time it gets loose is when the mind is in control.

It is allowed to leave its captivation but only temporarily to flow into our blood, to make us remember and recognize the fact that we indeed had the privilege to live those fantastic emotions. Ultimately, it is always important to distinguish the feelings of love from those of not accepting and being confident.

It is always good to trust that there is no shame to suffer after a breakup. It is always great to trust that there is no shame in being controlled by those feelings that were lived in the best atmosphere we had.

It is not a shame that those feelings stick to our hearts and soul and do not want to leave us.

There is no right or wrong in love.

Falling in love is different than love.

Falling in love is a process by which our heart is not owned anymore by us but rather by another one.

The lover's heart is like a magnet that sucked our whole existence into its world with its cocky smile.

I own you?

At the same time, our heart did not fight back.

At the same time, as if our heart loved the feeling of being sucked into the love world.

However, it is always important to realize that falling in love is nice; it is OK to suffer; it is OK to let go if we need to let go; it is OK after all, we have lived, loved, and embraced all the loveable emotions.

Live, love, suffer and embrace that life is a mixture of all types of emotions.

Learn to let go, but keep your soul surviving and waiting for the next mixture of emotions.

Written on 18 Feb 2019.

Desperate Relationship
or Live Alone

Human beings' personality strength level varies tremendously.

Our ego compliments itself by having the highest level of self-confidence, self-empowered soul, and a strong personality,

the personality that concurs against any obstacle.

The personality that can say no to people can say no to negativity and can say no to lovers who are not good enough for them.

However, and the unfortunate part is that: Two levels of people exist in this world

The person that accepts any partner due to the emptiness in their life despite the unhappy relationship.

The unconscious knows of this face that the heart needs the emotional empowerment offered by any person.

The unconscious is aware of the negativity imposed into its soul by the lover, despite the lack of emotional strength and fear of being alone with no source of attention and psychological empowerment, the soul becomes overwhelmed and cannot live alone with anyone

Such a person needs affection, care, and be with someone.

Because living alone for such a person is a significant suffering.

The moment this happens is the moment his or her world collapses.

It is the moment when darkness hits its pick.

The strong personality claimed over these years unveils its mask

It reveals the inner soul found inside.

The soul cannot survive a moment alone due to the lack of strength and confidence, due to the lack of being able to be happy without that partner.

The question lies behind all this: Is it possible that a strong personality cannot leave an unhappy relationship?

The beauty of having a relationship is not to fulfill our moments, not to make us happy, not to have someone who we can talk to every day, not to swim in a world of emptiness.

The beauty of having a relationship is to top up our lovely moments with new things, to have a peaceful mind, to have…

Why do we allow ourselves to be dominated by a partner for the sake of having a status I am in a relationship?

Such status is bringing happiness into a fake relationship.

On the other hand, there are those people who do not care to live alone because of them.

They have happy personalities.

Because for them,

Comfort is highly essential in a relationship

The support of the mind.

For such people, the level of self-confidence and strong character are dominating their lives.

Such people have no fear of being single, no fear of saying we are done, I do not want you.

They have no fear of taking actions although the person is so hot, so good-looking, and rich, but despite all that, they step up and take measures, and they tolerate no shit from the lover. They have the tendency to be happy even when they are single.

Their way of living depends totally on their ambitions and actions in life. A lover is always an addition to their life,

A person who flavors the pretty scenarios in their lives.

A lover for them is not a person that fulfills the emptiness in their lives; on the contrary, flourishes their lives with new things.

The new things that enjoy every moment every strength in this strong personality.

A fantastic friendship is a unity of two souls that employed their minds and heart in forming a strong bond.

The beauty that lies behind that bond is so pure and sincere to the point it flourishes itself in.

The lifespan of friendship nowadays is based on the strength of the bond built in every friendship, in every relationship, and in every family in this entire continent.

To have emotional stability is thought to be easy, but in reality, it is the hardest thing on this planet.

The question that lies behind this is why? Why we cannot be emotionally stable despite all the strength we have

Simple? The moment we consider our emotional stability is based on the friendships/relationships we built is the moment where the fragility of breaking that stability always exists.

Strength and Courage to Fight a Destructive Prearranged Marriage – A Story of Many

Have we ever asked ourselves what history lies behind the faces of people, we see every day? We can look at hundreds of faces daily, but what we don't realize is the fact that we are staring at hundreds of different stories in the history of those faces.

How many of those people have secrets in their past that have survived?

Secrets are born due to events created by human beings or nature.

How often is the secret exposed to the world by its owner?

The owner has the sole right to expose such a secret.

It has been experienced by him/her and only him/her.

Volcanos are always erupting in our minds from constant thoughts.

Worried, wavy blood is always roaming within the spaces of our hearts.

When does the owner expose the secret?

Trust build and break any wall built between two people.

The trust built between two new friends has allowed the secrets that are buried in the darkness to be exposed to light into freedom.

Someone has introduced me to a new friend.

I have never felt that a big secret has been hidden behind this face and soul.

Before continuing, I would like to say.

It is amazing how someone's secret can make him/her strong or vulnerable.

Building trust with this new friend was quick.

Recently, the mind and heart of this person decided to free the buried secret to me.

I have to point out that in the ideal Middle Eastern (ME) society, marriage is life.

In the ME, society doomed our lives with the idea 'We have to get married!'

Here it goes…

A special day introduced me to one of the most unusual stories I have ever heard.

A story of strength and courage.

A story where a person indirectly was pushed to jump into an unknown life just because society depicted this fact!

A story where a person supposedly had to meet their soulmate from a prearranged marriage just because society has depicted the presumptuous fact that we have to get married.

The strength and courage of this person were partly hidden inside the soul and partially built from the experience of the different actions occurring throughout this marriage.

Ironically, deciding to get married due to what society has depicted on us, especially at a young age, has been prevalent in the me society. Believe it or not, this decision sometimes could be destructive in our life.

However, as I always say, take every experience and look at it positively. What is the positive outcome of such a choice that led to a destructive life?

The positive aspect is turning the destructive decision into the most powerful one at the same time.

Why do I call it destructive and powerful?

I describe it as destructive because once we realize what we thought we would obtain from a marriage turned out to be the opposite, it led us to dive into darkness.

Our whole mind and soul start rejecting the fact that this is not what we believed in, and this is not the reality, the reality is what I dreamed of being.

The destructive state of mind continues until our strength and courage wake up from their dormant state, start fighting back, and accept the unexpected reality.

Then, we can move from the destructive to the dominant state.

Here comes the reality of what happened with my friend.

The destructive state has bombarded my friend's soul and shocked the whole state of mind.

But proudly, I would say, my friend's strength and courage Were so alert to the point they took over in an instant.

It took over the ignorance and deception of the destructive state caused by a non-human being.

It was caused by what was supposed to be a soul mate.

Indeed, life has hit my friend in different aspects, but self-confidence ruled all the deception.

At this point, my friend's mind started taking control of her emotions.

The life of this person entered the world of building a family.

We, as human beings, enter the world of marriage with high expectations of the perfect husband, kids, family, and thus life.

In reality, marriage could be a mixture of all but also could be just one adjective, misery.

This is indeed what this person's marriage started to become from the early stages.

This story revolved around a friend whose marriage turned from expectations of building a happy family to a miserable one.

This person started feeling that the soul is locked and condemned to die in prison.

The prison is made up of an artificial happy life.

But what people did not know at the beginning is that this artificial happy life was filled with negativity and chaos caused by a heart filled with hatred.

By a heart filled with low self-confidence and pride to cause misery and blame on his/her partner.

My friend's heart was filled with the unknown of when freedom will kick in and when it will come back.

My heart and mind were sitting in front of my friend with ears all wide open.

This person's mouth was telling me a story that I only thought would exist in movies.

This person's heart is filled with courage and strength to have survived this harsh marriage at a young age.

Many actions occurred throughout the years.

Society's eyes kicked the green light of staring at my friend's soul, trying to captivate every piece left of it being alive.

Society's weird, unacceptable mind always blamed a woman for a doomed marriage.

The selfishness and pride thrown by society members were beyond explainable.

All the people around my friend wanted her to stay in that marriage.

Some accepted her wish to divorce but under certain conditions.

All those were roaming around my friend's life, but no one, in reality, cared what her heart wanted except her heart and mind.

Strength and courage for a better life controlled the actions of my friend's heart and mind.

Over the years, her ears were sheltered with the most unsettling words. Over the years, her eyes witnessed the truth lying behind those faces around.

Over the years, court sessions, fighting with family, friends, supposed soul mates, and others, except for really

few events/people in her life, all tried to rule her world or keep her world in the destructive, darkest place.

Many years passed by when so many volcanos erupted in her life. Many years passed by when the divorce seemed near but far at the same time.

However, in the end, those events were splashed with the strength and courage she had in her mind and heart to reach her ultimate goal, divorce, and freedom.

In short, after all her struggles, my friend ended up with a great victory.

Victory of a free soul.

Divorce

A word pronounced and acted upon a lot in this century.

Too many thoughts evolve around the idea of divorce. People tend to lean toward accepting it. While others tend to see it as a taboo, especially for women

From my family's experience, in the beginning, while growing older, I have always felt that I am against divorce just because society depicted this fact.

Only because society back then enforced the idea that it was a shame to get a divorce or live in a divorced family, especially in the Middle East

However, with time, I started supporting divorce.

The question behind this is: Why it is shameful to get a divorce?

Why do we have to think twice about what people would say?

True, it is hard to get a divorce.

True, people have to think more than twice to get a divorce, especially if kids are involved.

However, divorce is not a shameful thing to do

No one wants to get married, so they get divorced.

The deplorable thing is to stay in a marriage where its outer layers are covered with fake beautiful moments.

The worst part is to keep acting that the marriage is lovely while deep down, the darkness has killed and buried every beautiful memory and moment to the point of explosion leaving behind all those bad moments.

At that time,

The shameful thing is not having the courage to say it's enough; it's time to split.

Many human beings tend to live for society and not for themselves.

They are willing to suffer big time, so the community does not point its fingers at them.

It is essential not to forget that those people in those societies are probably facing the same problem and have been covering their life with fake positive stuff.

Most of the time, people tend to get married based on the past and present lovely moments being experienced and lived.

They might have thought of building a great future together, having kids, and building an exciting happy life.

However, many people forget that married life is not all about butterflies and amazing honeymoon days but also about obstacles that could hit at any time.

It is not bad though because life by itself is not perfect, and we need bumpy roads so we can become stronger.

Marriage is not always perfect.

Married life resembles a road trip.

However, the roundtrip in this case never ends.

The journey is so long that it never ends.

The journey could take us to different places.

However, during the journey, the roads are not flat and smooth all the time.

They could be bumpy; there could be holes, rain, or thunderstorms during the journey.

Yet, in the end, moving forward is the key objective.

Marriage is not always about butterflies.

Many married couples say the butterflies and strong love fade away with time and only respect is left.

Is respect enough to keep the marriage alive?

Only couples can answer this

When divorce kicks in.

Most couples get married based on the butterflies and excitement they lived and are living, forgetting the fact that those are temporary, and marriage is beyond those things.

Do people take a moment and think about how their life would be after 15 years when all the excitement vanishes, the burdens of life arise, and the routine hits?

I believe successful marriages are those that involve two people who understand each other, who faced problems before marriage and overcame them, who know the worst part of their partner's personality but accept it, and who know that their partner is a strong person, who analyses things before taking action and who is prone to negotiation and many other things.

To say all this does not mean that marriage is a bad thing; on the contrary, I do believe in the best of marriages, and it is great to have kids and a great life.

However, before getting married, all of the above should be considered.

We should not get married just because society depicts this.

There is no age for marriage.

Why do we have to get married before 30 or 40 or 50? Who says so?

True, sometimes to have kids, females need to get married before 40; however, there is no particular age for marriage.

Probably, many who are reading this would be against it but take it from another perspective

Because society expects people to get married at a particular age, many couples are rushing into marriage, and thus, the divorce rate is increasing.

I have heard and witnessed stories where couples are married but in open relationships.

I have heard and witnessed stories where the man or woman has cheated many times, but the wife or husband had to stay in the marriage life just because of what society would say.

There is no shame in getting a divorce if the right reasons are there, and couples have tried to solve the issues, but they did not work out

Sometimes, we have to say; it is time to let go.

However, divorce should not also be something like I wake up in the morning, and I decide to get a divorce.

Counseling should sometimes exist; there is no harm in trying to fix things if things are fixable and not extreme.

Live your life in a peaceful way.

If you feel you have to end the marriage because it is suffocating you,

If you think you have to finish the marriage because you cannot live under the same roof with your partner.

If you feel you have to end the marriage because you no longer accept being cheated on.

If you believe you have to eradicate the marriage from existence because enough is enough.

Then, this is alerting.

However, to reach the stage where you're thinking about divorcing, you need to give it a chance and try counseling.

Divorce has always been at the far end of the road.

To reach, it means you had tried so many solutions before you decided on divorcing someone.

Eventually, it would be best if you lived for yourself and not for what society thinks.

Get married whenever you are ready and hundred percent confident,

We and only we decide if we want to get married or divorced.

Our life is owned by us, and only us.

Yet, always try your best to solve the problems before any decision

Ultimately, if the issues are not solved and the marriage has doomed your life with misery, then do what makes your soul free.

Revealing Inside Thoughts by Using Only a Pen and Paper

Happiness visits us occasionally.
Sadness knocks on our door surprisingly,
And sorrow cannot be kicked out of our lives easier.
People have their way of getting rid of the darkness capturing their lives.
One of the best ways to do that is by writing;
For me, writing is the cure for all the tension and thunder surrounding my life.
The treatment for all the madness.
Writing is the reflection of the feelings found inside;
Writing allows the inner darkness to reflect on a tiny piece of paper by using simple words.
A small piece of paper has the capability to absorb all the darkness.
Writing converts the tension into relaxation.
Writing is not only a tool to relax from all the miseries, but it is also a way to spread inspirational words into this universe.
It is nice to jot down all the happiness found inside on this tiny piece of paper and to share it with your beloved ones.
Weird how only one pen and a piece of paper can abolish all the madness capturing our lives.

Strange how only one pen and a piece of paper can reveal to the whole world our inner thoughts.
If writing is not a cure for you, then try something else; always look at the bright side of everything.

Frozen Hand in a Lovely June

92

Hello, my lovely June, beautiful with all your dark moments.

My dear June, many thoughts and feelings were implemented during your neighbor month in May.

My hand always craved for the pen to engrave what was going on inside me.

Are you afraid that nothing is left for you in my heart and mind?

Are you jealous? It is why you closed the door in front of my writings as revenge!

Oh, my lovely June, spray me with some magic so that I can write again.

Please, I need you to wake up my thoughts and emotions.

Awakening them will bring back life to my soul.

I missed holding the pen and writing on a tiny piece of white paper.

While writing, my hand used to run ahead of my thoughts and feelings.

Now, I will leave you, hoping that I can dig into writing once again.

Power of Qualities

Strength, confidence, motivation, perseverance. These qualities and others should build themselves inside you

The time this happens, conquering the world will be easy.

Holding these qualities will make people think twice before attacking you in one way or another.

A good personality contains all these qualities.

People should be careful not to let egoism control them.

Being confident will attract others toward you with curiosity to explore you and check who lies behind all this confidence.

Being motivated will drive your days with the enthusiasm required to achieve your goals.

These and many qualities are the assets of a successful life

Saying all this to you my reader is not enough.

There should be something inside you willing to do great things no matter what happens.

Never allow anything to banish you from this universe.

Always seek the best. Written on 2 July 2009.

Dreams

Dreams are part of our lives.
Dreaming about things keeps us surviving.
Always set dreams as life priorities.
No matter where you end up.
Just remember that you have done so many things in your life,
To lay down your arms is a big shame.
It will stay with you forever,
It will build itself in your consciousness,
Living life without dreaming would make us useless.
Living life without dreaming takes us to a boring place.
Our dreams live for us,
We live for our dreams.
To give up on them would be an embarrassment for us;
After all, we have come to this life to succeed and
accomplish our desires and dreams.
All of us are free to dream;
It is one of the things that no one can control.
Whether we are young or old, no one has the right to take
away our dreams.
Now, I am leaving you with your dreams and continuing to
follow mine.

Hope

Hope holds a huge meaning.
It is what keeps most of us surviving in this universe.
The hope of accomplishing our dreams,
The hope of having bright days,
The hope of diverse things,
We always work to make our dreams come true.
Our efforts may fade with time; however, hope revives them once again.
Why do some people lose faith in life and never regain it back?
Would it be at that point they lose hope in life and see the future as an empty box?
What happens when we kick hope out of our lives?
Hoping indulges us with the power to continue our mission.
Hoping makes us excited and allows us to feel that certain things still can happen;
This particular possibility keeps us fighting and surviving.
Everybody owns the freedom to hope;
The prettiness of hope is that not only one person owns it.

There were times in my life when my dreams passed into dormancy, but hope had always wakened and showed me that it is worth being part of life.

Written on February 2009 and 9 August 2009.

Jealousy

An undetermined power, found in every person.
Most importantly, do not exceed the red light.
Lovely when it is used as a love sign,
But sad when it exceeds the red light.
Most of the time, it is a clap of thunder that destroys
everything it encounters.
Jealousy, what wakes it up?
Is it due to love?
Is it due to hatred?
Is it due to money?
Is it due to envy?
Jealousy is the beginning of the end.
Is it reasonable to be jealous?
Is it wrong not to be jealous?
Jealousy is not bad when it stops at its limit.
Jealousy is a symbol of love and adornment in a relationship,
Jealousy is found in every one of us.
Control is the trait that keeps the jealousy buried inside.
Oh, jealousy, how much you can influence a human being's
life.
Oh, jealousy, should people be afraid of you and be in
constant wonder due to the power you hold?
Until now, jealousy did not force me into an ugly situation.

Sometimes, jealousy leads to foolish acts, which in the future build regret.
No words can describe jealousy's power, and what it can do to people;
In certain situations, it eats the person and takes his/her mind to the uncontrollable action zone.
Enough talking about jealousy. It has enough credits of fame.

Written on 19 Feb 2010.

Weakness

Many people have a trait of weakness as a permanent property in their personality.
Is it shameful to be weak?
Only when being in love, weakness will offer its pleasant aspects and put some taste into your personality.
Never in your life fall into the bad aspects of weakness.
If you do, life will boil your soul with no remorse.
Denying the weakness found in you would be lying to yourself.
It is always there, but most of the time it is hidden.
Depending on the strength of the personality and the situation in life, weakness may appear.
During these times, the control trait should stand up and keep weakness out of sight.
Being equipped with strength will abolish weakness.
Never allow it to take up residence in your life.
It's enough talking about it.
There is no need to spoil it more. Written on 21 June 2009.

Joy

People live their life to be happy.
The instant you enter into its house, a fantastic seeking will vibrate inside you.
This happiness will grab us into another world.
Suddenly, all the body organs start functioning fast as if they will explode. At this moment, problems will enter into a deep sleep with no return.
Without any doubt, money brings happiness, but is it the only source of pleasure?
Collections of incredible things yield joy
What a wonderful feeling it is
Your stomach starts cramping, yielding goosebumps
You see life from a whole different perspective.
There exist times where our happiness reaches its peak
Going back to its zero levels is not possible since it lost track of going back.
Shivering inside flavors our emotions with some beauty.
Will we ever get married to happiness?

Written on 19 May 2009.

Lebanon

Born since a million years.
Craved by many people.
The proudness grabbing my heart for you energizes me with strength.

The sweet home country, why are you overflowing with problems?

The sweet home country, what should we do to relieve your pain?

Beloved home, my soul is all yours.

Please don't give up on us, because we will not give up on you.

Your seasons confirm that you are the best country they have ever been part of.

My country, you are one of the smallest countries in the world

Despite that, your incredible nature reflects its beauty on the whole universe making it the most beautiful country ever seen.

The mountains stand there protecting the sea as if they are its guardians.

The Sea with its vast blue color keeps its blue eyes toward us.

The purity is always emerging from your ground.

You are as delicious as a unique cake where its recipe is vague.

Your archeological places enlighten you with the power to grab tourist's.
Intellectual people are present in you.
Your intellectualism and beauty engraved your name on this Earth
Born in our home country, Lebanon.
The country that sucks our soul inside its cave.
The country that has a high ego where it believes that we are its prisoner.
Years pass by where you might not escape from its captivation.
We get suffocated and cannot think when the chance arrives to flee to another country.
We have escaped
But!
No matter how much we resist its magnetism.
No matter how much we get bored with its physical appearance,
eventually, we will fall again in its arms and still be its prisoner
The home country already engraving all our loved ones in its heart.
As much as we try to kick out all our inner thoughts and feelings toward our home country, we will end up feeling the warmness
In the end, we have written history in our home countries.

Written in 2008.

Distance Introduces Emotions of Missing

January 19, 2012, no matter how far away I am,
My heart and mind will always be with you, my lovely
family, friends, and country.
My enthusiasm to see you once again grows more and more
with time,
It is the enthusiasm that never sleeps.
It is the ambition that separated us,
The aspiration that rises the pride in your hearts,
The pride of knowing that I'm doing a good thing in my life.
Life has put distance between us.
Saying goodbyes have always been part of my life
But the worst one was leaving you all, from December 17 till
Jan 9…I was part of the lovely dream…vacation in Lebanon.
The lovely dream that always has to end;
Now, I am back to reality, the Reality that cannot be described
as harsh, but at the same time, cannot be described as lovely.
I said my goodbyes and welcomed 2011 in Lebanon;
wonder where I will end up at the end of 2012.
Wonder what 2012 will offer me. I have to wait and see.
For now, I can say I am already missing and love you all.

Impact of Emotions

TOday, 27 January 2012, can emotions fade away within a few days?

Emotions enter our lives in just a few seconds.

Emotions are so stubborn to leave our world, taking time to do their actions.

Most of the time, every kind of sentiment has to end.

Would we be stubborn and try to keep those lovely emotions in our hearts and lives?

Imagine life without any dark moments.

Would it be lovely, or should the dark moments sometimes hit us?

Once we overcome these harsh moments, we grow emotionally and mentally.

Harsh moments make our personality and self-confidence stronger but…since people are different,

The ending story of the dark moments will differ from one person to another.

Some cannot handle any unlovely situations and fall into the dark world

And those who just overcome it easily,

But the question behind all this is…why this difference exists.

Is it because some people have no confidence in themselves?

Has nothing else to do in life besides craving what they have lost? February 19, sitting in the small, tiny room with the eagerness to continue writing this little thing.

Life, as I always describe it, revolves around many different situations.

Situations we wish will stay with us forever, situations that color our lives with happiness,

The happiness constantly searched for,

The joy that drives our inner emotions to the craziness,

The craziness to grab and make sure that the cause of joy will never escape from our mind, heart, and thus lives.

However, there are times were unexpected moments that may kill our glee,

May ruin the beautiful moments we had, lived, and wished to continue.

At that point, we think that life has ended for us.

Feel that nothing is worth living for;

Every lousy moment has captivated us literally in its cage

With no sense of misery.

With no remorse,

Every single moment spent in those black lights ruins happiness.

Again, the question is lying behind all that.

Is there any solution for all those ignorant, bloody, dark moments? Is it hard to believe that our self-confidence will overcome all the obstacles, no matter what?

Is it that easy to surrender for what life has just obliged us to face?

Aren't our lives worth struggling and fighting to make it lose the spell cast by the dark, stupid events, and for us to flourish with lovely, amazing moments?

Are we so drained to neglect the beauty and excitement of what the future will offer? And lock ourselves in the present. Surrendering alone will ruin anyone's life.

Blindness will destroy every special, unique, and beautiful moment that was supposed to fill our hearts with purity and lovely times, that was supposed to relax our mind, stop tiring it with constant thinking of why this has happened…why my life is like that…what will happen to me in the future. Why I cannot change it by only using a few words…the list can be continued forever.

Family, relatives, friends, lovers, and strangers bring happiness and sadness into our lives.

Any person, disregarding our family and relatives, whoever it is, from wherever should not allow his self-confidence to shake at any point.

Should not make our happiness turn into misery and constant worrying;

That applies only in the case when we are not the blamed ones.

Stupid, we are if we allow that to happen.

The suffering of losing that person is worth spending time on her/him, rather than spending our whole life feeling the same thing.

It is better to think that our mind is surrendering to the situation, has no strength to handle it anymore, and is starting to lose consciousness, due to all the tiredness coming from constant thinking.

Or to sense the hotness coming out of our hearts, all because it started to melt, begun to fade away in those dark moments, trying to ruin our beautiful life?

For me, it is not worth it to lose my mind or/and heart,

Both should be protected with every tiny piece of the soul we have left.

It might sound dull what is being said.

People reading this might say, "Mentioning it is easy but applying is much harder."

True that this is all not easy, but again by thinking deeply about it,

No one would love to live those again: Ignorant, harsh, dark, stupid, and finally, bloody moments, every couple of months or every day.

I would rather live them once and struggle with everything I have, to get rid of them, even though it takes me months on allowing them to enter my life anytime, and ruins it always.

Finally, different personalities exist in this world, and I accept that, but will never admit that a reasonable person won't have the strength to revive the strong qualities he/she has to overcome any situation affecting his/her life.

NEVER, EVER SURRENDER AND THINK THAT THIS IS MY DESTINY…

TRUE THAT WE ARE DESTINED SOMETIMES, BUT FOR OTHERS, WE MAKE THEM.

Spring

What a wonderful season it is!
The sleeping trees and flowers are waking up from their dormancy; putting some beauty in the place.
Spring is one of summer's essential glows
Sun emerges from its silence.
Sprays its beautiful smell into the surrounding
Rivers floating more slowly as if they are waving to us.
Everything starts to change as if the universe has changed its profile.
Life becomes more active.
Oh, spring! Do you have any lovers?
Your fabulous presence attracts lots of people into your arms,
Your charisma gets more potent than the year before.
Always stay generous with us.

Written on 20 May 2009.

Summer

A **season that is adored by most people.**
Spring has wonderfully prepared nature so that summer won't look bad in the eyes of the people.
Beaches wear their makeup expecting many visitors.
Mountains enjoy summer since many people visit them to stare at their beauty.
Vacations are the key dominant idea roaming in people's minds during this season.
The sun gains more power lightening the whole planet
Clothes start to fall off our skin, leaving a place for tanning.
A brown color forces itself on our skin but what a lovely thing it is doing.
Nightlife becomes one of the season's essential things.
It is impossible to escape from summer because it is like a magnet that pulls you toward it.
People wait for summer as if they are expecting a considerable gift
Oh, summer! How amazing you are.

Written on 23 and 24 May 2009.

The season's physical appearance influences the human being's way of life.

Entering into autumn encourages the human's mental state. Nature starts losing its skin

Trees and flowers become naked.

Despite all this, the beauty found under that skin compensates for all the prettiness that has fallen.

Sweet weather pushes you into a world of incredible feelings

Yellow beauty engraves its soul into nature, enabling us to enjoy it.

Although people start wearing more clothes, nature gets colder than before.

Clouds are on their way toward our sky.

Toward the most fantastic place ever witnessed.

Autumn is the beginning of many students' educational life.

Dear autumn, offers us three astonishing months washing us with happiness.

Written on 23 May 2009.

Winter

Calling it the most powerful season is not an exaggeration
Rain falls rapidly.
Roads become wrapped with icy water.
Clothes become ruined with no replacement for them.
Bad moods become the worst enemy for everyone.
Thunders send their evil toward humans.
Wait a second.
Is winter that bad?
Is it easy to forget all its beauty?
Do not worry my winter season, lots of people support you?
Winter's sweet weather with its coldness obliges us to approach and warm each other.
Imagine the sounds of our hearts when we meet during the warming process.
Heat will escape from our bodies into the surrounding
As if its main target is to protect us with its warmth.
The beauty of sitting all together in one room dominates every single house.
Clouds approach each other forming one population
As if it is guarding us against outer space.
Snow falls on the mountains.

Standing there on the sleepy trees and roads with its smile brings life to everyone and attracts tourists.
Don't you think winter's advantages abolish its disadvantages?

Written on 19 May 2009.

Sweet Place

Few meters but what a marvelous place it is.

Trees swing smoothly, releasing a sweet sound as if they are singing.

This place is continuously shining like a huge diamond attracting people to come and see it.

Flowers stand there and talk to each other.

Flowers form a lovely architecture and bond that brings a smile to the place.

Birds are flying over this beauty.

As soon as they cross the exit borders, they lose their wings and fall to the ground.

Staring at it, you can observe love, beauty, and purity.

Taking off your shoes when you enter is obligatory so that the crystal green ground is not ruined.

Unconsciously, people will walk with their naked feet because their fear of ruining this treasure is enormous.

The sun offers its brightness over the whole place, allowing the river to glow with its blue transparent color.

Diving in this river kidnaps you to an attractive cave packed with potency.

There will be no sound inside you saying, "This is a cave bursting with danger."

As soon as you step in,

You will instantly be captivated by its beauty.

A sweet place, you will always remain my favorite despite the running years.

Written on 15 May 2009.

Sea

Massive, isn't it?
Always Sparkly.
Its waves move in all directions.
Partly sending its hellos to us.
Slightly looking at our faces in a shy way
This gigantic thing has three faces:
One in the morning when it wakes up, either in a bad mood as
on the stormy days or good in the shining ones.
One in the noon where it is ready to embrace us with its arms.
One at night where it glows due to the moon's reflection as if
it is being pampered by it.
Its huge deepness can fit all people.
Staring at it brings life to me.
You can't escape or run from it.
It is like a magnet that sucks you inside its love.
It is the most relaxing place I have ever witnessed.
Whenever you are near, it vaporizes all your troubles from
your body.
Filtering your quandaries starts as soon as it captures you.
Releasing your inner thoughts to this immense blue place is
one of the best things you will do.
It will listen to you with its big heart.
Imagine it cares about us this much.

Words lose their meaning the time you bump into them
Always glowing, even in their darkest moments.
You are an enormous, lovely thing.
Thank God, you exist in our beautiful country.

Written on 17 May 2009.

Offering a Hand,
Helping People

To help the needy, humans should have a great heart and willingness to give something of their own to others.

Having the intention to help others is wonderful.

Helping nobody is a shameful thing anyone could do.

Imagine we have no shelter to sleep in.

We stay wandering the streets or picking a small corner to sleep in.

Let us go far with our imagination; tell me what will happen to us if we stayed without food for many days.

Many times when the food is not available during lunch

Our stomach starts screaming for it.

The most important thing to do is to help sick people.

Offering life for anyone powers you with happiness for what you have done.

I hope that someday, I can help many people through my organization.

Imagine the smile in their eyes, thanking you in a way as if you are the most crucial person on this planet.

You will get more than what you will give.

The smile cannot be purchased because no money in this world will be enough.

To watch the smile drawn on their whole body makes me shiver.
Living this life without helping anyone would be useless.

Written on 22 May 2009.

Traveling

Many countries that exist on this tiny rounded map,
My personality is eager to visit them all.
Traveling to other countries filters the mind from
all the troubles mingling inside.
Exploring different countries enrich us with knowledge and
experience.
Meeting other people opens your heart to the outside world.
Being thrown into foreign countries will indulge us with
confidence to rely on ourselves.
Traveling with someone or a group will spray us with
excitement, anxiety, and happiness.
Entering the airport makes me very glad.
Getting on the plane traverses me to another planet.
Landing in a foreign country opens my eyes to the vague
world.
It exploits my heart and mind with new insights about life.
It develops my soul in a bizarre lovely way.
Traveling just opens our eyes to new people and things that
we never had while raising up in our home country.

Believe it or not, spending money on traveling is worth a million times.

Written on 30 June 2019.

Saying Goodbye and Hello

Few times in our lives we are obliged to leave our beloved ones. Incredible how life is!

It was my first visit to Armenia where I spent awesome moments.

After two weeks, the time has come; separation became real the separation!

It was like an explosion occurred inside me and all my body organs stopped functioning except my tears which were falling like raindrops and thoughts moving in a dynamic motion pumping outside my head.

It was like the end of the world.

I tried to stop my tears, but it was like you, wanted something and could not reach it.

Like you are falling off a mountain where you were alone calling for help.

When I was in the car, I felt very hopeless; in a way, I wanted to stay in that small house, but at the same time, I craved my beloved home.

It was as if I was physically present in the car while my heart was kept with them.

When I looked into their eyes, I could not hold myself; it was as if someone has died, and I will never see this person again.

I wanted to control my sadness and get over that situation.

The mind has stored the memories of them.

When I call memories, they explode in my head and the pictures take me to the special memories

To the special moments, I spent with them.

I am sure there will be many moments like this.

To control emotions in such a situation is very hard

After all, we are human beings, filled with feelings that want to get out in one way or another; whether good or bad.

Despite all that, the feelings lived during that visit are worth way more than the separation itself.

Deep down, when we are separated from our beloved ones, the voice inside will always believe that reuniting should not be an option but rather a fact.

We have to think and make sure we will meet again.

We have to engrave in the planning of the meeting again once we board that airplane.

Years passed by, and the excitement of the thought that I will feel the love of my Armenian relatives is awesome.

The day has come.

The moment arrived when the airplane Armenia's Arms welcomed the aircraft.

Finally, it has landed.

My whole body was ready to embrace all my relatives.

The moment has arrived to smell the origin of the Armenian people again.

Going outside the airport, and what a beautiful view I have seen.

My eyes were all over the place trying to find my relatives.

Few more minutes and these eyes will be relieved.

No more wondering. No more closing them and trying to remember how my relatives looked and the moments we enjoyed.

Now, these eyes, this brain, this heart, this body,

will be relaxed,

With few more steps to take with the hands ready to hug them

and feel the beautiful emotions.

Finally, kisses and hugs were spreading in

this lovely atmosphere.

All our hearts were pumping.

Wait, there was still one more moment to witness,

The moment when we reach home as more of my relatives

were waiting there.

Those fifteen minutes seemed like one hour.

Many thoughts passed through my mind in those minutes.

What will they do now?

Are they glad that they will see us?

Now, the moment arrived when we had to enter the house.

Now, again for the second time, the hearts started pumping

immensely

No more minutes to spend on the road.

No more wonderings.

Going out of the car, opening the door, and seeing them.

For the first time in my life, it seemed that I have never left

Armenia.

It seemed that I went out for a few hours and came back to my

home.

All the excitement that was born for the first meeting after

five years has disappeared,

Now, standing there in front of them.

It has been five years since my eyes did not see them.

Hugs, kisses, and laughter were spreading in the atmosphere

at that beautiful moment.

Many days started passing by when stories were told.

Many days passed by and they included happiness, joy, laughter, and love.

In a word, amazing emotions only were part of our lives at that moment.

New people were being introduced into our lives.

The more we spent moments with them, the more we loved it 15 days passed.

Now the moment came when we had to say our goodbyes.

Impact of Real Friends on
a Dark Day

Being in the UK, away from home introduces many thoughts into your mind.

Being away from home explodes your mind with the most stupid but essential questions, with no sense of knowing the answers, except when being kidnapped by the situation.

Sickness hit us without any prior notice;

Disregarding it is out of the question,

Not being afraid of the situation, especially in the killing sickness would be stupidity by itself.

What makes the situation tough is the fact that the family is far away,

Away to the point that dying from pain will be the only resort, rather than waiting for someone from the family to arrive.

So only the sickness, your body, and the four walls standing there are your last moments,

Four walls are watching you without bothering themselves to help or feel your pain.

You are alone in that tiny room,

Alone with nothing except your pain and thoughts of what kind of ending is this.

But…

Never underestimate the friends you have.

True that family is far away,
True that you should be afraid when pain and sickness try to kidnap your life,
But again, never forget the meaning of friendship.
One phone call, made my friends run leaving behind everything.
Run to make sure that the ambulance would be there quickly.
Friends reaching me and feeling my pain.
Friends holding my hand, trying to comfort me in any way possible.
Friends physically not there, but mentally and emotionally connecting with me, making sure that I do not feel alone.
The simplest things they have done brought power and belief into me, in those horrible times,
They have empowered my weakness with strength.
Their tiny sentences gave me enormous happiness, believing that I am not alone.
No matter how far you are…you will always realize that friends will be the support in your happy and sad moments.
Always trust that the friendships you are building are worth having,
Those friendships make your life better and enjoyable;
Very important not to forget that you are the support for them too.
Selfishness in friendships will destroy the lovely moments spent together,
Selfishness in friendships will make you lose track and end up alone in deserted places with no sense of emotional support.
To listen to your friends' problems and consolidate them brings joy to your life.

The satisfaction of knowing that you are, taking away some of their pains,
Holding some of their burdens.
Friends do not only share enjoyable moments, and spend time together, but also to kidnap their miseries from them.
By doing that, less burden will remain on them and more on you, but
Eventually, friends are found to share the sad and happy
Moments, or else selfishness will succeed in owing you and destroying your friendship.
Friendships should be very pure.
For me, a friend is like a sibling, A good friend is considered part of my family.
Always use honest words rather than coloring the honesty with beautiful jargon.
No matter how bad the honesty sounds, use it.
Now, maybe friendships are not the same for everyone;
perhaps friendships for some people are just a matter of spending time and having fun.
Just remember how you will feel if a friend ditches you at your worst moment.
Friendships are the support in our lives;
Never forget that.
A TRUE FRIEND BRINGS JOY TO YOUR LIFE IN YOUR HAPPY AND SAD MOMENTS…

2006 Basketball Arab Championship Winners "Wonderful Journey to Morocco"

Traveling is one of the best things in life.

The day has come when we had to travel for the Arab Championship.

Excitement pushed itself into our lives.

Waiting for the airplane to take us was one of the most prolonged moments I have ever witnessed.

Knowing that this trip would be great was a reality, but many surprises occurred.

Heading to this destination has put some thoughts in our minds concerning the place and the Arab Championship.

The flight took us to our target which is holding the cup for the second time.

After six hours of flying, the airplane landed.

I had an instinct that the cup was waiting for us to come, grab and take it back to our beloved country, Lebanon.

Our emotions lived together under one roof.

Lots of beautiful moments were spent at breakfast, lunch, and dinner.

Laughter was being spread in the rooms freely every time we gathered.

After our first wrong step, losing against the Tunisians, anxiety barged into our souls.

Wanting it or not, nervousness has stayed with us until the last moment,

On the other hand, the power of controlling these emotions was enormous.

Days have passed, and the smile on our faces has never left us alone.

I was confident that our team would reach the final despite all the obstacles.

Almost everyone didn't want us to win.

We had our eyes on the title, cup, and gold medals.

The last night before the most crucial day in our lives, as we went to bed, I am pretty sure that everyone prayed to God to win the final.

Lots of emotions from happiness to anxiety were mingling inside.

A few hours, the name of the winner will be announced,

The little voice inside me assured me that the title is ours.

Getting into the game with all the pressure on everyone was not easy.

Everything was done for our team and beloved country.

This small country which is suffering a lot has engraved its name into all the Arab houses.

Playing against the group to whom we had lost the first game indulged us with power and made us more excited as if we are entering into a battle that we must win.

The 40 minutes was all we needed to wear the gold medals, be the source of attention, and raise our names and flags into the sky.

I can't explain the things happening inside our minds, heart, and body as if we had just been born into this life with no clue what it was all about.

One second we were sad, and the next we were happy.

It is the first time in my life that contradictory feelings of anxiety, happiness, sadness, and amazement had walked with me during the whole 40 minutes.

Our weak emotions couldn't take a single break.

The last minute has arrived, and everyone is running behind the title

30 seconds left; the ball is with the Tunisian team.

At that point, our hearts dropped, and our excitement became paralyzed in front of what is going to happen.

Are they going to score?

Are we going to lose?

Please no, we have to win, our emotions will not be able to tolerate a loss.

We have to raise Lebanon's name and flag high…

Unfortunately, 20 seconds left, and the Tunisian team scored

Now, we are down by 2 points, what shall we do?

At that point, our anxiety hit so high.

However, the game is not over.

We are a team built on the basis of stubbornness to win and do our best to win on such occasions.

Now, the ball is with us, the ball is moving from one nervous hand to another, and the ball itself became nervous and cannot anymore tolerate the stress mingling between those hands.

Now, the ball is with Emma from our team, and here you go,
13 seconds left, and Emma what bravery, shoots from three
points.
Oh my God, guess what happened, our eyes could not
believe it. Oh my God, you cannot believe what happened!
Emma scored three points.
And on top of that, she got a foul, wow.
Now, is the time for Emma to have nerves to score this one
shot that will increase our chances to win the title.
She has done it.
Suddenly, being down by two, our team got the lead by two.
We were at the edge of losing the title.
The excitement inside us pushed us unconsciously to all start
jumping together with no control.
We thought that we had won; it was over.
Unfortunately, the game had not yet finished,
13 seconds remained, and time was ticking; the ball was in
the Tunisian's hand.
Four seconds were remaining, and the Tunisian shot three
points.
Here, as if the world has just stopped.
Wondering whether this shot was going to enter or not.
If it did, everyone's dream would die.
If it didn't, an explosion would happen.
The decision lies within this orange ball and ring.
Here is the moment that everyone was waiting for.
The ball refused to enter
The adrenalin exceeded the peak line.
Pushing us into moments of insanity.
We started running left and right with no control.

Hugging each other was one of the most beautiful instances in my life,
You can see all the smiles on our faces.
You can feel your heart pumping fast as if it will explode from happiness,
You can watch the tears on our faces going down with vast confidence and without shame.
Now, for the second time, the title is ours.
We enjoyed our time a lot.
Going back to our beloved country.
The moment we left the door of the airport, a massive number of people from fans, families, and journalists were there applauding and taking pictures.
Everything was like a dream.
The team resembled a huge. Heart filled with courage, desire, love, and unity.
All the players from those on the court to those on the bench were awesome.
I will never forget this journey in my whole life.
Every memory will stay in my head no matter what.

Written on 25 and 26 May 2009.

Basketball! UK

I have always been part of the Lebanese championship league.

The University of Manchester acceptance letter brought a dream of playing basketball in the UK.

Basketball has been part of my whole life.

The University of Manchester Women's basketball team

Arrived in a new country, city, and team.

Been introduced to new people.

None of them I have ever met or heard about

Different people from different nationalities

And all were there to form a team.

To create a team with the hope and ambition to raise the University of Manchester's name high.

A new mission was introduced into my life.

The mission of practicing and playing hard is to raise my university's name high.

Indeed, this is not a Lebanese team, but eventually being part of something means full dedication to it.

Every win brought with it happiness into each person's heart.

The pleasure that we are succeeding.

But at the same time, the losses have been accompanied by the desire and effort to work harder.

To work harder for the sake of our teammates

Our team and thus the University.
Those losses had brought selfishness into the
upcoming games,
The greed of wanting to be the first no matter what
The desire to enter the court as if we owned it.
As if we have built a wall around it not allowing or letting
anyone hold it with their winning.
The losses introduced excitement to our lives and colored our
team with harshness.
The sweet harshness of playing with our full soul and wanting
to crash the other moments with as many points as possible.
Having to play away games brought laughter to our lives.
The laughter spread on the bus.
Despite the tiredness, what counted is the time we
spent together
The time that will never be part of our lives again in such
events
Now after many months.
The end has approached.
It is the end to say goodbye to this lovely team.
I do not know how the last practice will feel.
I do not know how the last game will be.
All I know… for now is that the past few months have brought
amazing, lovely, joyful times.
Going to the first training, throwing myself into this unknown
place into many different people's lives.
The first game against Liverpool, the away game.
During that game, I felt the beauty of those moments and
believed that future times with those people would form great
events that will be buried in my memory forever.

The first Leeds game that flourished our team's soul with the eagerness to crash every team.

The game awakened and fired our bad basketball side.

The side that has hit our brain with the reality that we need to step up and fight more while playing for the sake of ourselves and the team,

Our thoughts from that point have changed.

Our ideas sound harsh.

Our beliefs have become the enemy of all other teams

There was no more space for being sweet in the upcoming games.

Saying that sounds harsh, but the eagerness to raise our team's name

High was and still is the primary thought swimming in our minds.

Our aim has washed away the meaning of harshness and replaced it with the ambition of winning and qualifying for the sake of our efforts and the University.

The end has approached.

Everything can be summarized as follows.

In the beginning, it was us being strangers to each other.

In the end, it is us being friends with each other with lovely buried memories that will live in our heads forever, and never die.

As I always have said everything eventually will end.

Two more weeks and the goodbye becomes reality.

But the only thing I can say besides goodbye to this team

Is

Welcome to the new people in my life.

It has been a great, fantastic, joyful experience that will be added to my historical basketball experiences.

I hope you enjoyed reading this!

Written on 27 and 29 Feb 2012.

General Quotes

Jealousy lies within the holes found in the unsatisfied heart.

Everything will go away. Nothing stays forever. Memories are lived and died, leaving behind memories and scars that made us learn and evolve.

Love is an emotional beauty empowering our life with sweet happiness.

Empowering ourselves with love is an unconscious act, impersonating our thoughts with imaginary love is a conscious act full of stupidity.

Breaking the silence inside our hearts is an act full of confidence.
Life is a story of adventures.

Capturing the light found in our life is dependent on our mindset.

Jumping into the unknown flourishes the heart with
adrenalin and excitement.
Don't be afraid of the unknown; be scared of being fearful of
the unknown.

Welcome the negative moments with an open heart and
show them the beauty found in your happy free soul.

Thanks for reading!

If you may have some query regarding the book or want to
send me a feedback, you call always contact me on my email
at: jessy_gh8@hotmail.com

www.ingramcontent.com/pod-product-compliance
Lightning Source LLC
Chambersburg PA
CBHW051310250726
48656CB00004B/1576